I Rode a Bike for 50 Years

Memoir of an endless 1974 bicycle journey across America

Konrad C Nau

Non-family and non-friend names used in this book are fictitious. Any similarity to real persons names, living or dead, who may have encountered cross country bicyclists in 1974 is coincidental and not intended by the author.

Disclaimer: Reading this book does not guarantee the good health, good fortune and good strangers needed to complete similar adventures. The author recommends consultation with your primary care provider, your local bike shop, and an experienced route planner.

Paperback ISBN-979-8-9917795-0-0

Hardback ISBN-979-8-9917795-1-7

Library of Congress Control Number: 2024921991

Cover design by Rony Dhar

Printed in the United States of America

This book is dedicated to Luella, Taylor, Indi, Maddox, Quinn, Jaxson, Maize, Waylon, Rainey and Cormac.

May you always seek adventure, be kind to others, and oh yeah -ride a bike.

Table of Contents

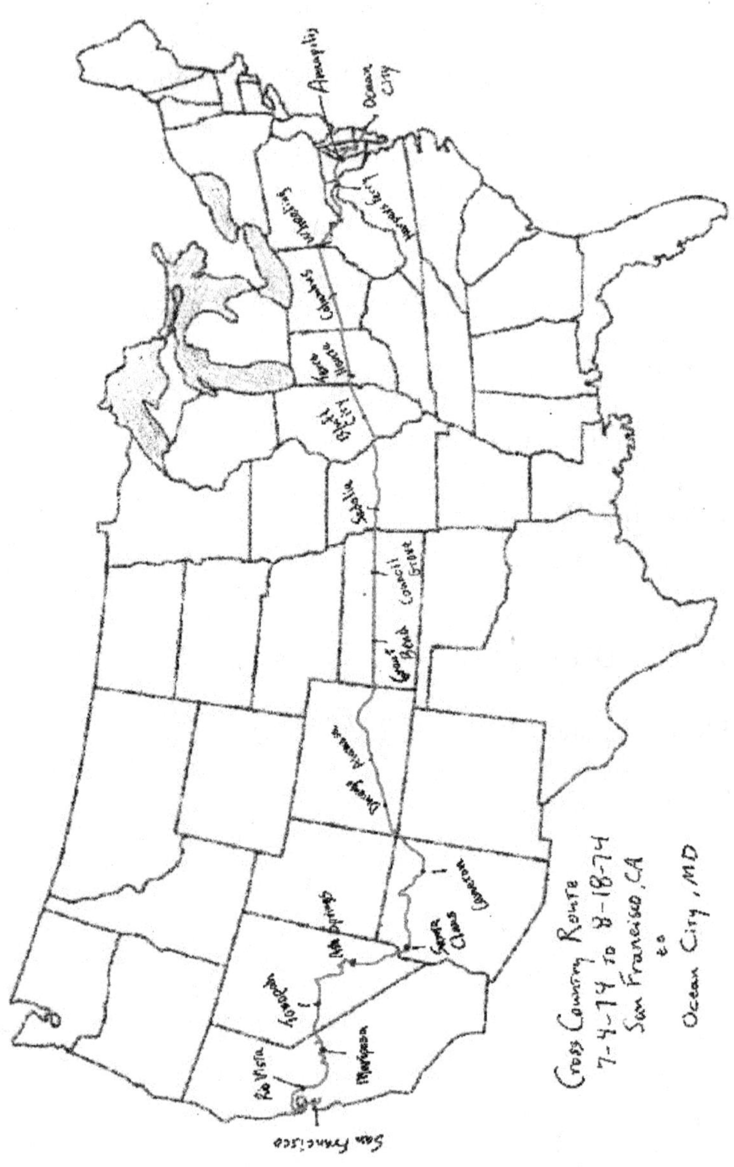
Cross Country Route
7-4-74 to 8-18-74
San Francisco, CA
to
Ocean City, MD
San Francisco
Rio Vista
Mariposa
Council Grove
Sedalia
Columbus
Annapolis
Ocean City

Author's Note

There is a destiny that makes us brothers:

None goes his way alone.

What we put into the lives of others,

Comes back into our own.

Poem by Oregon's first Poet Laureate, Edwin Markham, Circa 1901

Pinned to a wall in the Alamosa Fixit Shop, July 1974.

Sometimes you experience something that affects you for the rest of your life. You may not even know it at the time. It can be something traumatic, or something randomly wonderful. It can be something in-between. Either way, you eventually look back and see how that experience or series of events changed you – the way you look at yourself – how you see others – how you perceive where you live. Fifty years ago, this happened to me when I rode a bike across America. In many ways, I rode that bike and those experiences for fifty years.

You are about to enter the world of my 1974 cross-country bicycle trip and my 2024 research and reflections. Dates, places, prices, food, distances and destinations are exactly as written in the journal that I wrote in at the conclusion of each day. All descriptions of bicycle mishaps are precise; however, my comparison to a professional cyclist may be a bit of a stretch. All encounters with people along the way actually happened. My journal contained many direct quotes, but I do not have a fifty-year echoic memory for every word of my conversations. Parts of memoirs are said to be works of creative non-fiction, meaning that I had to create dialogue that reflects the likely tone and tenor of conversations that I couldn't remember verbatim. I have used the real names of most friends and family members, trusting that this bond will prevent any legal action against me (just kidding). I used pseudonyms for the many other folks who enriched our journey. If you recognize yourself in my writings but feel you were misquoted or misunderstood – my bad. Sorry about that. All historical and 2024 references were extensively researched, and I endeavored to specifically credit the source of any direct quotes from the writings or songs of others.

Chapter 1

1974

June 28

Wheeling, West Virginia to Pittsburgh, PA: 50 miles by car

Pittsburgh, PA to Chicago, Illinois: 410 railroad miles

June 29 - July 2

Chicago, Illinois to Oakland, California: 2,438 railroad miles

So, what was it like 50 years ago Papa?" Yeah, actually, none of my 10 grandchildren ever asked me this. But granddaughter Lulu graciously informed me that I didn't "look as old as a grandfather," and Indi relieved me by saying "You don't smell old, Papa".

Then there was Jaxson in one of those rare moments at the end of a chaotic day where a child lays on your lap, looks up with their baby blues and connects with you. "Your face is smooth Papa." But I knew that it was getting harder to shave every one of those scraggly hairs from my evolving turkey neck.

I do, however, have something that looks and smells old, yet still survives - the journal that I kept on my coast-to-coast bicycle trip that my friend Bob and I took in 1974. When moving from West Virginia to Colorado I found it in the bottom of a box that I packed up six house moves ago. Now retired, I had the time to peel back the faded packing tape and to discover what was so important that caused me to drag this box house to house. I opened the bound blue cloth covered Bell Telephone Laboratories journal with its maroon leather corner protecters (obtained from my ex-wife's father who worked at the New Jersey Bell Labs). The stiff paper crackled, and I paused at the first turned page.

Cross Country Bicycle Trip

Summer of '74

Coast-to-Coast Journal

What was 1974 like? What was I like? What's changed and what has remained the same – for better or worse? When I look back 50 years would I find something thought provoking or head scratching? What was funny, humanity reaffirming, or foretelling of my future life? How many details had escaped me, and how many times did I think or write things I can't believe came out of my mouth – or pen rather? Well, as I turned the pages, I found all of this and more.

Who knows what compelled me to undertake a grand adventure? There was no prize or notoriety to achieve, no personal loss or tragedy to recover from, and no corporate or financial sponsorship. It's been said that having a grand adventure and being able to tell tales about it is essential to manliness. Maybe there's a human gene for exploration that gets activated in one's twenties. More likely it was a large measure of sensing this might be last time in my life that I would be able to do something like this. Perhaps I was seeing the course of my life on a map and fearing possible detours, but at the same time seeing detours never taken as adventure lost.

There was a 1960s song by Mel Carter called *Hold Me Thrill Me Kiss Me*[1]. It often played at the end of CYO dances at St. Vincent's gym when you hoped you were slow dancing with a cute girl and not standing against the wall looking on with the rest of your pimply-faced peers. Although singing of first loves more than adventure, there was a resonating lyric "Don't be fooled thinking this is last you'll find". I couldn't heed the warning in adventure or in love. I was fooled thinking that this was my last time to accomplish something big – before the caliper brakes of time and reality slowed me into the next big turn in life. A cross-country bike trip would eventually come to an end - but future adventures awaited me. So too did marriage to my first love Jill come to an end - but I would find new love. Both experiences would change me for the better. The English explorer Sir Wilfred Thesiger said "the harder the adventure the way worthwhile the journey"[2] – so why not bike coast-to-coast then get married two years later?

We were in two different colleges, Bob and I, and although growing up in the same parish, grade school, and high school - we were two very different people who shared a love of bicycling. I don't recall whose idea it was, but we developed this notion of a future bicycle tour across the USA. Bob was built more like Lance Armstrong (pre-steroids) and excelled in charging up hills. I was built like a taller Greg LeMond. As a distance swimmer in high school, I took the long-haul steady cadence approach up hills. Charging downhill was my forte. We were both from large families and a bit on the quiet side. Bob pursued an accounting degree, while I was a pre-med biology major.

We were fully caught up in the Bicycle Boom of the 1970s and had even licensed our own basement bicycle shop as teenagers along with our friend Robert (aka "Bookstore Bobby" because he manned the lunchtime book and school supply store at Central Catholic High

Me on the left, Bob on the right

Wheeling Intelligencer photo by Andy Leheny

School). Our intention was to use our commercial license to purchase high performance foreign bicycles and repair tools at dealer prices from Stuyvesant Bicycle

Distributers in New York City. We wanted to learn how to take apart and rebuild or repair all parts of a touring 10-speed from derailleurs to building wheels from a hub, a rim, and a box of spokes.

Although I cut my teeth on an $80 Schwinn Varsity Sport 10 speed, it was a monster weighing in at 38 lbs. without packs or racks. We set our sights on British built Falcon bikes almost 15 lbs. lighter, with double butted 531 tubing, Campagnolo derailleurs, Wineman brakes, and glue-on tubeless tires. Mine was a metallic emerald color with chrome front fork tips. Boy, did we have a lot to learn.

Our hours spent in the basement Anybody's Bicycle Works (named in honor of the counterculture Anybody's Bike Book by Tom Cuthbertson), gave way to growing-up things like college, summer jobs, girlfriends, and the military draft. In 1972 the prospects of being drafted and sent to Vietnam seemed to be lessening but still lingered in the back of our minds.

Bob's draft number was 221, and my Selective Service draft number was 120 the following year. By the winter of 1973, President Nixon's end the draft campaign promise came to fruition. Although the draft lottery went on until 1975, the last men drafted had lottery number 95 and the birthdate of July 20, 1952. Without the threat of military conscription, my friend Bob and I spoke of the coming summer of 1974 – the one between Junor and Senior years of college - as being our last chance.

So, after a few pitchers of beer, Bob and I foolishly and firmly committed to bicycle across America in the summer of 1974. That year created Americana in several iconic categories. Top 40 radio songs were Band on the Run by Paul McCartney and Wings, John Denver's Annie's Song, and Elton John's The Bitch is Back. Blazing Saddles was my number one movie that joined Godfather Part II and Towering Inferno as box office leaders. The board game Dungeons and Dragons was released in 1974, while a Hungarian architecture professor was quietly inventing the Rubik's Cube. A gallon of gas cost 58 cents and the average car price was $4,400 on an average income of $12,840. McDonald released their enduring marketing jingle "Two all-beef patties, special sauce, lettuce, cheese, pickles and a sesame seed bun". Skittles, Kraft Singles, Ragu spaghetti sauce, and granola charged on to the food scene. If nothing else, 1974 was a banner year for fast food and junk food.

1974 was also the heart of the Great American Bike Boom. In the 1950's, bicycles were sold mostly for kids ages five to fourteen, and rarely for people over 16 years old, as the lure of the automobile was irresistible. Few people rode bikes on roads outside of town, but as baby boomers came of age themes of healthy exercise, and a clean environment emerged. Then almost overnight, bicycle sales hit 14 million with almost 60% being sold to adults. So, it was in this 1974 world that two young men from West Virginia set out to pedal across America, and I was lucky enough to be one of them.

On June 28th Pop drove us from our homes in Wheeling to Union Station in Pittsburgh. I said goodbye to my father at the train station. He must have wondered why he ever gave permission to his not yet 21-year-old eldest of seven children to do this.

"Goodbye, Pop. Thanks for everything, and don't worry we'll be safe and stay in touch," I said getting a bit choked up.

"Bye, KC. Be safe," he stoically replied. We didn't say 'I love you' very often in our family, but I certainly felt it.

Like Meriwether Lewis, we started our Expedition in Pittsburgh, Pennsylvania.[3] (William Clark joined them in St. Charles, Missouri). We boarded the overnight train from Pittsburgh, Pennsylvania to Chicago, Illinois with gear packed in paniers, sleeping bags and tent in stuff sacks. We were on our way to the Pacific Ocean with our $138 Amtrak tickets. Our bikes were shipped ahead of time to the motel in San Franciso.

Bicycling coast to coast did not become popular until 1976 when 1,750 cyclists joined the Bikecentential'76 event pedaling from Astoria, Oregon to Yorktown, Virginia. I had seen a small ad in a bicycling magazine where a guy named Clifford Franz advertised that he could provide maps for anyone doing a long bike tour. The price was right at ten dollars, and with a stack of his maps our journey was plotted in highlight green. In 2024 the Adventure Cycling Association (with a membership of 50,000) is selling a TransAmerica Bicycle Trail Map Set for $189.00. We were an oddity in 1974.

In Chicago we boarded the Amtrak Zepher and headed across the Midwest plains and the Rocky Mountains. Glenwood Springs, Colorado was a stop on the Zepher that I must have slept through – not knowing that this place would play a big role in my future. Besides being the home of a famous million-gallon hot springs pool, Glenwood Springs is served by Valley View Hospital, where my son and I would both work in 2017. I think our eyes are often closed when God shows us a glimpse of the future. But my eyes were open as the train pulled into the Oakland, California Amtrak station near midnight. We had endured almost 4 days in coach class, trying to sleep upright, walking back and forth between train cars, and living on dining car food.

"So, where are you guys staying before your big bike trip begins?" asked John, a fellow train traveler we had gotten to know.

"At the Ocean Park Motel in San Francisco," I replied, having personally made this, my first ever motel reservation.

"You do know that the train station is over 10 miles from that part of the city?" he queried with raised and weary eyebrows. "How are you planning on getting there?" he asked, already sensing a naïve and unprepared answer.

"I guess we'll call a taxi," said Bob, as John's long face registered a very definite 'No plan – I knew it' look.

In the first of many acts of kindness (or perhaps pity), John informed us that he happened to live in San Francisco. Soon we had been graciously and safely dropped off at the Ocean Park Motel on 46th Avenue. Thank God, as I was having second thoughts about the odds of two Pittsburgh Steeler fans surviving a midnight taxi ride through Oakland after Franco Harris's 'Immaculate Reception' of 1972 with 22 seconds remaining that eliminated the Raiders and propelled my Steelers to the Super Bowl. Raider fans are fanatical and notoriously poor losers.

The Ocean Park Motel was San Francisco's first motel in 1937, and in 1974 was your average low-mid budget lodging. Their website now notes that at the time, J Edgar Hoover denounced motels as being 'dens of iniquity' and 'camps of crime'. Little did he know that this motel would become a 2024 Art Deco Landmark demanding many multiples of the room fee he would have spent.

Standing on the cool brown sand at Ocean Beach we stared into the rolling surf and blue waters that disappeared into the horizon. After some sightseeing and briefly jumping into the cold Pacific waters, we would spend the next 45 days pedaling America's backroads.

My 1974 Ocean Park Motel Post Card

Bicycles have changed a lot in 50 years, but the backroads really haven't. Did you ever notice that most paved roads have a white line painted along the sides of the pavement? The outer white line is formally called the Edge Line Pavement marking, but initially it was the "fog line", helping cars stay in their lane during foggy conditions. It turns out they are made of paint or thermoplastic laced with reflective glass microbeads, hydrocarbons and a variety of noxious heavy metals. Like many safety measures, white lines were later found to have unintended consequences - like accelerating erosion of the underlying asphalt.

Nonetheless, we often rode on the white line conveying respect for the motorist. A visual communication that we're just pedaling from town to town and didn't mean to impede anyone. The fog line also offered a Zen-like meditative focal point when I was in my pedaling cadence zone. While hiking, Cheryl Strayed called this zone her "primal gear void of anything but forward motion". For me, the white line was where I could feel the rhythm of cycling, the push down and pull up of the pedals, the breath and the pulse, and the feeling that this effortless effort could last for hours. It could even take me across America.

Riding to the right of the white line put us on "the berm" – clearly out of the traffic lane. It is here where one entered the imaginary world of safety from becoming roadkill. But beware, it is the land of pavement diversity and flat tire roulette. Territory to the right of the white line was always an adventure. The FTR ('Far To the Right') declaration of most states in 1975 functionally relegated bike riding to cambered gravel and glass strewn berms more often inches wide in areas with broken pavement requiring tightrope steering.

Ah, then there is bicycling to the left of the fog line. Stray too far to the left of the white line and you were unarguably in the car lane and fair game for honking, "get the F_ _ _ outa the way" greetings, near sideswipe brush offs, or a direct hit. But when the road was downhill and clear of traffic, invincible speeds were reached to the left of the white line. Our only physical contact with the road at 40+ mph was 1 square inch of tire rubber per wheel. Left of the white line was where I truly felt the magic of what happens to you on a bicycle. Richard Ballantine in his 1972 Richard's Bicycle Book said it so well, "...you experience the tang of the air and surge of power as you bite into the road...the clouds and the breezes. You're alive! You are going someplace, and it is you who is doing it."

Looking back, I think I strove for the rhythm and guidance of the white line on the road of my career, but eventually I saw it crumbling some of my asphalt. Now, I fondly remember those precious moments of riding to the left of life's white line – at invincible speed, alive and going someplace – because 50 years ago -I rode a bike.

Chapter 2

Ode to Thomas Stevens

July 3

San Francisco, California: 0 miles

Sleep was fitful on the night before we started our journey. So unusual for me as I typically fall asleep one minute after closing my eyes, and I don't mean just after sex. It's not as if we were vying to become the first or fastest humans to bicycle coast to coast across America. The honor of being the first was earned 90 years earlier by Englishman Thomas Stevens in 1884. We shared a large measure of his determination, yet very few of his challenges. Stevens accomplished this feat in 103.5 days over 3,700 miles of a patchwork of macadam roads, wagon wheel rutted dirt roads, canal towpaths and railroad tracks. He was alone and relied on the kindness of others for most of his food and lodging.

In 2024 the cross-country speed record is held by the Austrian Christoph Strasser at 7 days 22 hours and 11 minutes over 3,000 miles of concrete and asphalt highways. Strasser was accompanied by a dedicated support team supplying him with water, food, and massages. We shared a large measure of his road conditions, but none of his ability to endure cycling past the point of delirium on 2 hours of sleep.

Neither of these amazing cyclists chose the shortest coast to coast route of 2,460 miles from Santa Monica, California, to Jacksonville, Florida. Nor did Paul Stutzman in 2010 when he biked 4,951 miles from Neah Bay, Washington, to Key West, Florida, in 69 days. We shared a large measure of Stutzman's encounters with many fascinating people, yet we did not have his time to travel. Our route would cover 3,558 miles from San Francisco, California, to Ocean City, Maryland, and we had only 50 days till our senior year of college would commence.

Looking back at these three incredible bicyclists, and comparing them to Bob and me, it is Thomas Sevens who stands wheels above us. Literally - his bicycle was a high-wheel or penny-farthing bike with a 50-inch front wheel. His Columbia model was quite expensive for his time at $100, had no gears, and

weighed about 50 pounds. Our Falcon models were a couple of hundred dollars, had 10 gears and weighed about 20 lbs. He packed a small but heavy tool bag (complete with a monkey wrench), a tin cup, coat and hat, a change of clothes, canvas gaiters (that would save him from a rattlesnake bite), pen and paper, and a revolver.

We only had a few items in common - my journal, a pen, and a change of clothes, a rain jacket, and a cloth bicycling hat (bicycle helmets did not become mainstream until 1985). Bob and I were compelled to lug 10 maps, Kodak instant cameras, an aluminum two pot/one pan alcohol burning cook kit, sleeping bags, a transistor radio and a tent with rainfly.

Stevens could not actually bicycle the whole route because of muddy unpassable dirt roads or rivers forcing him to walk sometimes even on railroad tracks through long tunnels or over icy bridges. In fact, Stevens had to walk almost half of his journey pushing his bike along the way. We also could not actually cycle our entire route either; however, our problem was mechanical bike and tire issues. In fact, we hitchhiked 590 miles in total catching rides in vans and pickup trucks mostly across desert. Still, we felt that our pedaling 2,968 miles qualified us for a legitimate cross-country bicycle claim.

Knowing the stark road conditions he would have to traverse; Stevens had planned on averaging 40 miles a day. He ended up averaging 36 miles/day even though he would have to push his bike on many days. In comparison, Bob and I hoped for a paltry 75 miles a day. We ended up averaging 71 miles/day counting only the days and miles that we cycled. We experienced the same awe with the mountains, desert, and plains that Stevens so eloquently described in his book Around the World on a Bicycle. Stevens was also already aware of the plight of our buffalo, and we mutually failed to see a single one.

Tragically the US buffalo herd was decimated from a 1600's peak of 60 million to only 325 in 1884. This was caused by the intentional slaughter of bison, critical to Native American life, to eliminate as many indigenous people as possible so that the West could be colonized by white Europeans. Even as a foreigner in our country, Stevens observed the sullen affect and expressionless faces of the many Indian groups who endured those shameful times, although he described them with some racially disparaging language in his writings.

By the time of our journey, bison recovery efforts were underway, and the buffalo population was up to several thousand, reaching 31,000 by 2019. In 2024 there are almost 21,000 Plains buffalo in conservation herds, 20,000 in tribal herds and many more in commercial herds bred for buffalo burgers and steaks. In 2016 the American bison was officially named the national mammal of the United States. Cool gesture, but little comfort to the buffalo and American Indians who previously enjoyed no such notoriety or respect.

Astonishingly, in 1884 Stevens only had to spend a handful of nights camping under the stars. He enjoyed invitations to sleep in homes, barns and hotels complete with free food shared by strangers enthralled by this intrepid man atop his towering bicycle. For most, it was the first time they had ever seen a wheeled vehicle other than a horse drawn wagon or cart. The Model T Ford would not travel on their roads for another 25 years. Small high-wheel bicycle clubs existed in many cities, and once he reached the Midwest, they treated him as a celebrity. Many joined him for a few miles as he pedaled through their town. We also were blessed by the generosity and curiosity of strangers in 1974, although we still spent most of our nights in a nylon tent and purchased most of our food. We enjoyed no real celebrity (outside of our friends and family) but we did have one cyclist ride with us near the Grand Canyon, and a front page newspaper story in the home town Intelligencer.

Like Stevens, we were never attacked or robbed by anyone. But unlike us, Stevens had to use a revolver on several occasions. Most notable was when threatened by an oncoming mountain lion. He aimed to kill but only struck the ground in front of the beast kicking up dirt and stones that scared it off. A badger and a prairie dog were not as threatening but did not fare as well. The bears that Stevens, Bob and I encountered didn't take much interest in bicyclists as they turned their heads briefly only to lumber away.

However, almost 50 years later while biking to work I rounded a bike path corner to be confronted by two black bear cubs running straight toward me. Because I was talking to my wife on the cell phone which I held in my right hand, I could only slam on my left handle brake (which you will recall works the front wheel). As I summersaulted over the handlebars I envisioned coming to a stop as the mamma bear prepared to devour me. I must have scared the bears more than myself as I ended up alone and embarrassed on the pavement. Decades apart we cross-country bikers faced different dangers and thrills but similar generosity and good fortune as we cycled across the America of our times.

After reaching the Atlantic Ocean, Stevens once again summoned his courage and continued to bicycle around the world. He was a beast! All we had to do was wake up July 4th and start pedaling to the Atlantic, then summon some courage to leave the idyllic world of the summer of 1974 and continue to our final year of college and the rest of our lives.

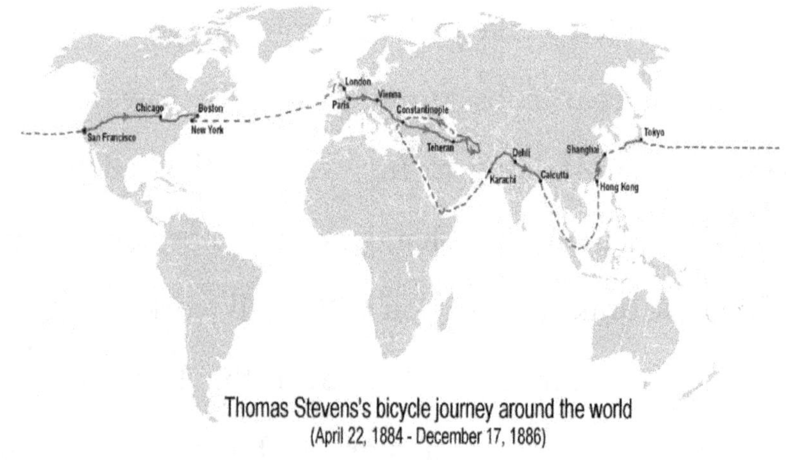

Thomas Stevens's bicycle journey around the world
(April 22, 1884 - December 17, 1886)

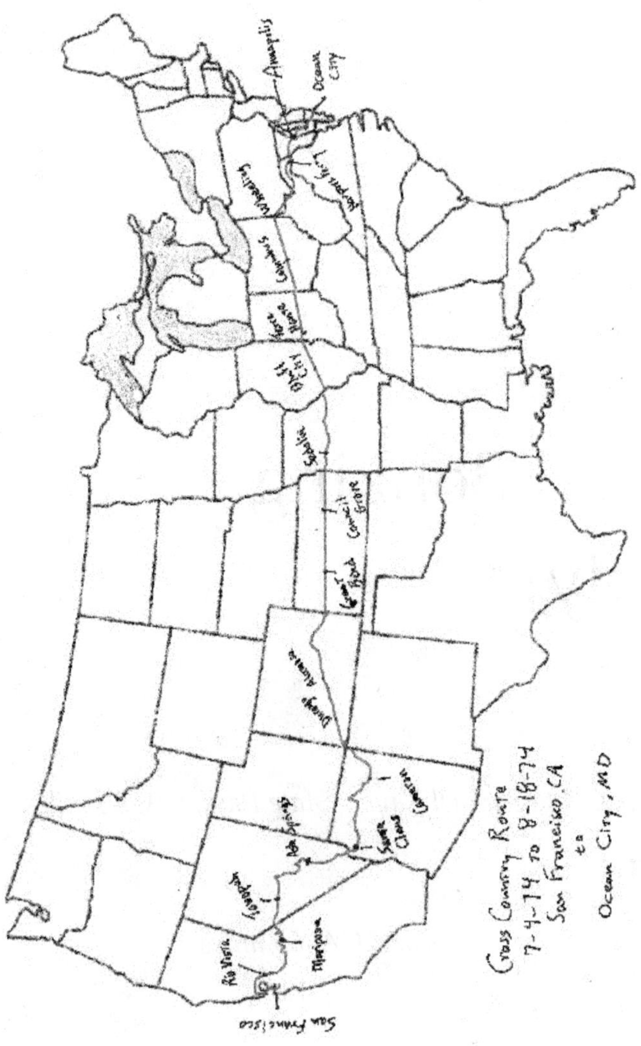
Cross Country Route
7-4-74 to 8-18-74
San Francisco, CA
to
Ocean City, MD

Chapter 3

Lost and Bonking Already?

Day 1 July 4

San Francisco, CA to Samuel Taylor State Park, CA: 50 miles

Day 2 July 5

Lagunitas, CA to Mankas Corner, CA: 65 miles

Dear reader, before we get started, please permit me to dispense with the tiresome whining of sore butts and the wind that plagues many stories about distance bike riding. In 1974 I wore a pair of wool blend bike shorts with a single layer of 'chamois' - the real thing –

soft, porous leather made from the flesh split of a sheepskin. In a rainstorm they felt like wearing a dirty baby diaper. I estimate that it takes 100 hours, or 2 weeks of 8-hour bike riding days, to toughen your ischial area soft tissues sufficiently to no longer have saddle soreness. Till then we used liberal amounts of Vaseline petroleum jelly. In 2024 my bike shorts have a nylon blend of triple layer synthetic 'chamois' that wicks away water and provides maximum comfort to my butt. This is good because like most old men, my buttocks are rapidly disappearing. Some just slowly vanishing, and some migrating around to my lower abdomen.

Now regarding the wind - headwinds just plain sucked the soul out of me and vanquished any sensation of forward momentum. Crosswinds were OK unless they were strong enough to blow me over. Unfortunately, my bicycle was not a sailboat. I was confined to narrow strips of pavement and could not tack across oceans of asphalt. Tailwinds were the best, especially the ones that I could not feel, as they pushed me along. They gave me a sense of newly found power and energy every time. So that's it. I shall not whine about a sore posterior or the wind for the duration of this adventure.

On July 1, 1974, with our bikes packed and stomachs full of cereal and sausage, we hit the road at 9:30 am. The mist of morning fog left droplets on the grasses and shrubs, but a clear blue sky was peeking out above. I tucked away the map as it looked like a short traverse of Golden Gate Park and then north to the Presidio would put us on the Golden Gate Bridge.

"Hey Bob, didn't we pass that pagoda looking building about 10 minutes ago?" I wondered out loud.

"We sure did. Are we lost already?" said Bob.

"Maybe a little. We just need to find our way out of this park and get back to the numbered streets," I confidently replied.

Fifteen minutes later after passing several small lakes and blossoming flower gardens we stopped to dig out the map. Our future wives would have stopped any passerby to ask directions – but we were guys about to weave a path across America and could not possibly ask for directions from a little old lady walking two toy poodles. That's when Jack pulled up beside us.

"Good morning, dudes! Where are you headed all packed up like that?" said Jack.

"Oh, hey, Hi! Today we're trying to get across the Golden Gate Bridge, then eventually to the Atlantic Ocean."

"Groovy, man. I'm Jack and I can get you up on the bridge. It's along the route of my morning ride," he replied.

Jack looked to be in his early 50's with a lean athletic build and some long hair hanging out from his short-bill biking cap. We found him to be gracious and unpretentious. He was, however, a prototype MAMIL-

the Canadian pejorative for 'Middle Aged Men In Lycra' riding outrageously expensive bikes. He pedaled the latest golden yellow Moleni Team Edition Colnago Super with sew up tires – comparable to a $6,800 2024 carbon frame Cervelo Soloist 700 cc Gold Dust. I suppose that I have become a COMIL (Cheap Old Man In Lycra) as I refused to pay more than $1,600 for a road bike last year that was quasi "custom fit" for me. I tell myself that my legs and butt would hurt even more had I not been "custom fit". Who knows?

"So what tools are you guys carrying?" Jack asked breathlessly as we climbed a short hill. After I rattled off our short list, Jack replied

"I can't believe you don't have a chain tool, man. You gotta have a chain tool dudes."

Although Jack's morning ride would take us another 7 miles to complete, we pedaled through beautiful neighborhoods and then to the Presidio where the smell of salt air welcomed us. The road finally led up to the massive color-conflicted international orange Golden Gate Bridge and we stopped to say goodbye to Jack.

"I have a gift for you dudes," he said reaching into his behind the seat tool bag.

"I want you to have this chain tool. Have an awesome ride, and may you never have to use it!" Jack was a godsend and an inspiration. He guided us through the maze of Golden Gate Park and got us back on course. We were no longer lost on day one.

Bob with Golden State Bridge in background fog

We paid forward a good deed by helping a couple fix a flat rear tire on the Golden Gate Bridge and enjoyed the wide bike lanes that we shared with fellow bikers with whom we chatted along the route.

Just as I was about to ask Bob if he thought all California roads had bike lanes they came to an end at Fairfax Hill where I learned about 'bonking'. As I pedaled up the hill, I suddenly felt exhausted, weak in the legs and a little dizzy. Bob would prove to be the stronger hill climber over the course of our journey, but he seemed to abruptly pull out of sight as I felt like I was pedaling in mud. Bonking is the result of depleting the muscle's glycogen, the chief fuel source of energy. I was so busy taking in the sights like a wide-eyed tourist that I forgot to eat and drink along the way. This was a daily marathon worth of exercise, and my fuel intake needed to convert from the three meals a day routine to regular and frequent eating and drinking. A few minutes of rest, a handful of nuts with a candy bar and a bottle of water restored me and I kicked myself for knowing better and having to re-learn the hard way.

We pulled into Samuel Taylor State Park and after pitching our tent and each downing a family-size can of Dinty Moore Beef Stew, we met up with some bicycle touring guys from San Diego.

"How did you guys plan your route across country?" asked the suntanned blonde surfer-looking guy as he handed us each a beer.

"We had our course mapped by a guy named Clifford Franz who sent us a stack of maps and some emergency contacts for only ten bucks," I replied

"No shit dude? That's who planned our bike trip too. We told him we had 2 months to tour the country, and he mapped out a big route all around the state of California! Do you want to know what he told us?" he asked with a smirk.

"Sure", said Bob.

"He told us to never ride your bike across

America – just stay in California!"

"Well, that's not great news," I muttered as I finished off a bottle of their Olympia beer.

Bob and I nervously laughed along with them, and with that wet blanket thrown upon our party we said goodbye and turned in for the night wondering what exactly made our route something "to never ride". We couldn't believe that the San Diego dudes didn't bother to ask Mr. Frantz why the made that statement.

Undaunted, we arose with the sun on Day 2, broke camp, and put in 22 miles to Petaluma, California. A one-inch pavement ledge, a closing pickup truck, and some road glass resulted in a big bang from my rear wheel. With a ripped sidewall and instant flat, I spilled onto the road. No damage to body or bike, but I already had one ruined unpatchable tire less than 75 miles into our journey. I got out the rim glue, and replaced the tire.

We purchased our cereal, milk and GORP

ingredients at a small grocery store with a 'No shirt-No service' sign. We had set a three dollar a day budget for each of us and we read labels and prices closer than housewives shopping for a family of ten during the 12.3% inflation days of late 1974. Whether you know GORP as "Granola Oats Raisins and Peanuts" or by the 1913 Oxford English Dictionary definition "to eat greedily", we substituted M&Ms for the granola and it was our sweet and salty, inexpensive, high protein, high fat energy food. GORP-like energy snacks in America date back to at least 1906 in Horace Kephart's Camping and Woodcraft guide where he writes: "A handful each of shelled nuts and raisins, with a cake of sweet chocolate, will carry a man far on the trail, or when he has lost it." In 1968 Harmony Foods got a patent on their combination of dried fruit, nuts and seeds called 'Trail Mix'. We found our concoction cheaper and easier to grab by the handful from the large zip-lock baggies we kept in our front panniers.

After climbing our last Pacific Coastal Range

mountain outside of Napa, we rolled into Mankas Corner at 6:30 pm hungry, tired and ready to break our budget. The only three buildings were a gas station, a Mexican bar and grill (which were told was for migrant workers only) and a combination deli/bar. The cute barmaid and sandwich-maker Julie seemed thrilled by our sweaty, dirty, not-from-around-here arrival.

"Julie, what do you recommend for two guys who just biked here all the way from San Francisco?" I asked with my best bad-boy bravado.

"A six-pack of cold beer and my famous roast beef sandwich," she replied without hesitation.

We talked with Julie about our adventures and the weather (no rain expected till October). Being the only customers in the store, the owner joined our conversation and ended up inviting us to stay at his house that night.

We met his young teenage son over morning breakfast as he prepared to go to work making dried apricots by cutting the tree ripened fruit in half, removing the pit and then placing them on wooden trays cut-side up to dry for three to five days in the sun. At 85 cents a box he was able to cut 8 boxes in 8 hours. That sounded like a lot of work for less than seven dollars, but he informed us that the migrant Mexican and Puerto Rican workers could cut 15-30 boxes a day because "they were built for that kind of work". That sounded like some racial BS to me, but I dared not offend our hosts. After all, I could not speak with any authority as I had never actually met a Mexican or a migrant worker back home in Wheeling, West Virginia.

With a parting gift of some delicious, dried apricots, we left Mankas Corner amazed and grateful for the generosity they showed us wheeled interlopers. Was this welcoming spirit why Clifford Franz told the San Diego dudes to stay in California? What would happen to us when we eventually crossed the eastern state line?

Chapter 4

General Delivery

Day 3 July 6

Mankas Corner, CA to Caswell Memorial Park, CA: 80 miles

Day 4 July 7

Ripon, CA to McConnel State Park, CA: 40 miles

We planned several mail stops along the way where we could get letters and goodies from home. This was accomplished through the amazing process of the US Postal Service called General Delivery. Like many ways to get free stuff and other valuable life lessons, I learned about this outside of the classroom in college.

"Larry, this is the last time you can receive your mail by General Delivery ", announced the middle-aged short brown-haired postmistress.

"You have to purchase a Post Office Box like the rest of the students."

"Come on lady, please.... It's not like I'm getting drugs or contraband delivered to me," pleaded the bearded long-haired college history major.

His faded green T-shirt and stained white painters' pants may have given him the look of an itinerant, which General Delivery was partially designed for, but it was a typical fashion for a 1970's college student.

"Larry, I know you can't have a child delivered to you or a human body part mailed to you, but even your letters and 8-track albums from that mail order place have overstayed our 30-day limit for General Delivery", she replied. The slightest grin was cracked as she tried to maintain her postal business face. She knew her post office trivia and how to use it.

This was the first time that I ever heard (actually overheard) about General Delivery. Staying in touch with family and friends along our route was a challenge. Collect phone calls home were an expensive burden to place on our families, and neither Bob nor I were big phone conversationists. General Delivery to small town post offices seemed like a good plan for us to communicate with folks back home. After food and navigation – predictable communication was important.

Article 1 of the US Constitution granted Congress the power to establish post offices and post roads which led to development and funding of many roads and highways across the US. Some of these postal roads would form our cross-country route in the summer of 1974. When the US Postal Service began in 1775 and for the next 21 years all mail was exclusively picked up at one's local post office building. Delivery of mail to personal homes began in 1796 for an additional two cents surcharge, and it didn't take long for people to test the boundaries of this federal service. In 1914 parents of a 5-year-old mailed their child to the girl's grandmother by train for 53 cents – significantly cheaper than the train fare. The Lewiston, Idaho, postmaster personally delivered the child to her grandmother. It took 6 years for the US Postal Service to officially ban the mailing of humans, but the Lewiston postmaster would typify the kind of down-home unique services that I would encounter in small-town post offices.

Rural areas only had General Delivery and rented PO boxes until October 1, 1896. Rural Mail Carrier home delivery would not begin until this date, in Charles Town, West Virginia - the hometown of William L. Wilson, the US Postmaster General and past president of West Virginia University. It is also where I would raise my sons and practice rural family medicine for 35 years.

This is how General Delivery works. For persons with no permanent address or those who have not yet purchased an official PO Box, the service of "General Delivery" still exists in some (not all) post offices. Large cities may route all General Delivery to a single regional office. Mail addressed to an individual name, followed by the words "General Delivery" and the post office town name and zip code will be held by the postal service for a maximum of 30 days. Individual post offices may shorten the hold days based on local storage capacity or other mysterious reasons left to their discretion. Personal ID is required and a "storage fee" may be applied at the discretion of the local postmaster. We chose 5 rural locations that had low populations and discovered that many of these post offices were one of only a handful of buildings in the entire town.

Our plan seemed like a good one, but we did not anticipate the day of the week or time that we would arrive in these towns. Our timing was perfect in Rio Vista, California, our first mail stop of the journey. After

Bob's General Delivery letters from home

a 25-mile morning ride we arrived at this town of about 3,000 people situated at the confluence of the Sacramento and San Juaquin Rivers.

Not much was going on there in 1974, but in 1985 Rio Vista was in the national spotlight when the 40-foot Humphrey the Humpback whale wandered off his Alaska to Mexico migration path, entered the San Francisco Bay and swam 50 miles up the Sacramento River to Rio Vista. He wallowed in the shallow river water and Marine biologists feared that the fresh water would damage his skin's ability to repel the salt water of his ocean home. Crowds thronged to see the whale and bought whale T-shirts and Humphrey souvenirs as they waited to cheer whenever he surfaced. After multiple failed attempts and emerging worrisome skin blisters, the US Coast Guard finally drove him back to ocean assisted by a flotilla of private boats upstream obnoxiously banging on metal pipes while a boat downstream lured him with recorded sounds of Hawaiian Humpback whales feeding. In 2024 a stone monument of wrong-way Humphrey stands on Main Street, and you can still dine on a pizzeria combo meal called the Humphrey Special.

In 1974, a few blocks from the future Humphrey monument site, we anxiously asked the postmaster for our General Delivery mail. He returned with only a single letter from my friend Ed and a single letter from Bob's mom. The long-awaited cookies and other family and friend letters didn't make it in time, but the postmaster assured us he would forward them to our next mail stop in Cameron, Arizona.

Headwinds made pedaling in the 90-degree heat

to Caswell State Park a struggle, but the shaded campsite among tall pines was worth the effort. A stealth Park Ranger silently pulled up to our campsite catching us by surprise as he walked up to our picnic table while we finished our 2 ½ pounds of beef stew and bread with honey dinner. After the usual explanations of who we were and what we were doing he got down to the more memorable part of the conversation.

"Where are you guys headed next?" he queried.

"On to the California Aqueduct Bikeway according to our map," I replied.

"That's a really desolate and windy area and I'd head due east to McConnel State Park near Cressy then on to Yosemite if I were you," he strongly advised while giving us one of those 'If-you-ever-want-to see-your-loved-ones-again' looks.

"OK then…. that's what we'll do," I replied, and he hopped back in his Park Ranger pickup truck and continued his patrol.

Sunday, July 7, was a day of rest. We left the park at 12:30 pm and rode with the wind at our backs toward Ballico, CA. We had a close call with the California Highway Patrol who caught us pedaling across the Stanislaus River north of Modesto on what was apparently a 'Bicycles Prohibited' Rt 99 Freeway bridge. After a barrage of questions, they learned we were from West Virginia and probably figured we didn't know what Freeways were. They concluded the inquisition with "Go ahead boys".

Once we reached our revised destination of McConnel State Park we took a swim in the Merced River where I had an unexpected experience. I had just gotten out of the water and was drying off when Bob and I noticed two kids splashing around and yelling. I just kept on drying off and Bob wondered out loud if they were playing or drowning. Well, it turned out the girl (10-12 years old) couldn't swim too well, and her brother was coaxing her back to our side of the river. She was hanging on to a tree branch and a Hispanic woman in the water told us in broken English that she could not swim across to get the girl. I grabbed the nearby life ring and swam across -surprisingly remembering all that Water Safety Instructor4 stuff. I talked to her a bit, got her in the ring, and towed her back across the river to her mother. After two summers of lifeguarding that was my first pull in – not exactly a Baywatch[5] worthy save in the surf, but I was feeling sheepishly proud. Meanwhile the little girl was getting what I assume was the Spanish version of the parental combination 'angry-you-did-that' and 'so-thankful-you-didn't drown' talk from her mother.

We cooked T-bone steaks, mashed potatoes, and corn on the cob for dinner. Boy was it good. That meal and the fruit given to us for free by a kid at a roadside fruit stand made this a memorable recouperation day.

Chapter 5

You go this way-
I'll go that way

Day 5 July 8

Cressy, California to Midpine, California: 60 miles

I suppose that we should have stuck together and not separated ways on Day 5. "Safety in numbers", "no man left behind" slogans and all, but it really didn't occur to us while we sat on the roadside as Bob replaced the first of many flat sew up tires.

"Crap look at this." Bob said holding up his

snapped in half rear wheel quick release skewer.

"You gotta be kidding me!" I said in disbelief.

"Looks like I'm going to need to find a bike shop and get a new one. I can't even ride with my rear wheel unattached."

Looking at our map I guessed that the nearest bike shop would be in Mariposa, 23 miles ahead in our direction of travel for the day.

Bob volunteered, "OK, listen, how about I hitch a ride and, get a new part and then catch up with you in Mariposa?"

"OK, I'll just ride on ahead and meet you there. It's a small town and I shouldn't be hard to find. OK, see you in a couple of hours" and I shoved off and pedaled down Rt 140.

There was no real discussion about contingency plans, what to do if Bob hadn't arrived in Mariposa by nightfall or anything resembling a consideration of the pros and cons of deciding to separate. Remember, this was fourteen years before I got my first cell phone- which was a Motorola Bag phone with a whopping 2.5 hours of talk time per battery. We had no arranged campsite and knew no one for hundreds of miles to the west and over two thousand miles to the east.

We had the naïve confidence of Lewis and Clark, who traveled separate routes on part of their journey back east from the Pacific coast. They parted ways at Traveler's Rest, Montana and planned to meet one month later at the mouth of the Yellowstone River. Now that I live part-time where their trail ended near the Lewis and Clark National Historical Park on the Oregon coast, I have learned that Clark arrived 2 days early and Lewis arrived 2 days late to their agreed meeting spot and date. The mosquitoes were unbearable, and Clark couldn't just sit and wait for Lewis. He left him a handwritten note on a pole explaining that they had arrived and then departed. They finally found each other one week after their rendezvous date -140 miles downstream from the Yellowstone River. This would have been a real problem for Bob and me. Absent this historical detail - we were clearly cueing up a future recipe for a Dateline episode featuring a missing West Virginia bicyclist/ hitchhiker named Bob.

Thoughts of serial killers, or drug and sex traffickers were not part of mainstream American's consciousness in 1974. Most of our nation was not yet forced to acknowledge and react to the possibility that horrible evil people were out there. Like Ted Bundy – the self-described "most cold-hearted son of a bitch you'll ever meet" – who was murdering in 1974 but was not yet fully identified or apprehended. By the time he was finally caught over 30 women and girls had been raped and murdered. It was not until 1989 that he would die by the electric chair.

Or like Jeffrey Dahmer who had not started his killing, dismemberment, and cannibalization of young men until 1978. After admitting "I knew I was sick or evil or both" he died in 1994 being beaten to death by a fellow prisoner.

Last, but not least, there would be John Wayne Gacy who did not start his killing and torture spree of over 30 men and boys until 1978. It was also in 1994 that he was executed by lethal injection with his last words being "Kiss my ass." We were fortunate in our innocence to not have worries about encountering devils like these.

But when Bob heard the slow gravel crunch of a car pulling off the side of the road behind him, it caught him by surprise, and he spun around with his heart up in his throat. From the black and white California Highway Patrol (aka CHiP) car emerged the middle-aged officer in his starched tan uniform with blue necktie, campaign styled brimmed hat and the Eisenhower style short olive jacket with shoulder patches.

"What seems to be the problem here, son"

Bob sauntered toward the officer with his side-to side sway, resembling but not exactly an "aw shucks" demeanor.

"I have a broken rear axle skewer and am trying to get to the bike shop in Mariposa. I can't ride my bike without one."

"Well, son, there is no bike shop in Mariposa and the nearest is 15 miles back in Merced," replied the officer.

Without alcohol I didn't know Bob to have the gift of gab or a salesman's personality – but he had the gift of sincerity and the almost unbelievable story of where we were from and what we were doing. Somehow the officer offered to drive to Merced, pick up the $6.00 skewer and deliver it back to Bob with roadside service. This action by a CHiP officer saved our day, as the kindness of others would repeatedly do so along our way.

I walked out of the shoe repair shop having paid $2.25 to have my bike shoe cleats nailed into place. After riding cleat-less so that a line would be worn in the leather shoe bottoms to demarcate the best location. I looked forward to their promise of increased efficiency being really locked into the pedal. It had been over four hours since we separated, and no Bob. On top of that we were nearing a week on the road and still had barely made it halfway across California. Suddenly,

"Hey KC! What's for dinner?" yelled Bob as he rolled down the main Mariposa drag.

"Man, I was beginning to worry about you," I replied, and we hit the A&W restaurant to ecstatically feast on burgers, fries, and their signature root beer in a frosted mug.

We sat only 100 miles from the spot where founder Roy Allen opened the first A&M draft root beer stand in 1919. After an early evening pedal up to Midpine, we pitched our tent in a clearing just off the highway. After being told numerous bear stories from the citizens of Mariposa, I decided to sleep with the frying pan and a large stick in the tent to scare off any hungry *Ursus arctos horribilis* (aka grizzly bears). I wondered if any campers were ever found mauled to death still clutching their stick and frying pan.

"We need to push up into Yosemite tomorrow, and I need to ask you a question," I soberly said to Bob.

"At this pace, do you think we can make it to Ocean City?"

Chapter 6

Beatles to Beetles and Ghost Towns

Day 6 July 9

Midpine, California to Crane Flats, Yosemite: 55 miles

Day 7 July 10

Crane Flats, to Tuolumne Meadows, Yosemite: 42 miles

Day 8 July 11

Tuolumne Meadows, Yosemite to Benton, CA: 75 miles

Day 9 July 12

Benton, California to Tonopah, Nevada: 70 miles

Day 6 to Day 8 rides up into and through

Yosemite National Park were our first real experiences climbing high mountain roads in the West. The 1970 Beatle song *"The Long and Winding Road"*[6] was the last #1 hit they recorded before their breakup later that year. The world's most famous band of all times would be legally dissolved in 1974, but that did not keep the lyrics out of my head as we pedaled from Midpine, California's 2,585 feet elevation up and over Tioga Pass at 9,941 feet. Besides, there were new melancholy 1974 albums by an independent Paul McCarthy and John Lennon that transitioned us into the new Beatle-less world (which would unfortunately be the disco era).

While writing in 2024 I listened to the lyrics of *"The Long and Winding Road"*[6], *"Band on the Run"*[7], and *"#9 Dream"* from my phone app. Unimaginable in 1974 when phones could only call other phones. I was acutely aware that I had certainly changed, and perhaps so too had the meaning of the words.

Seeing the printed verses conjured up specific

moments from those days in Yosemite. *"The long and winding road, that leads me to your door, will never disappear."*[6] We steadily climbed out of the hot and dry foothill woodlands whose scant winter snowpack is barely enough to nourish the scattered blue oaks and grey pines. As we passed through the Arch Rock entrance we entered the lower montane forest. The sweet spicy smell of pine tree terpinol filled the morning air and the forest thickened with diverse deciduous and conifer trees. Another 10 miles of salty sweat and pumping quads and we were in 'the valley'.

The magical Yosemite Valley at 4,000 feet with Half Dome and Yosemite Falls was as breathtaking in 1974 as it was for several return visits I would make over the next decades. The perseverance and foresight of Frederick Olmstead, Galen Clark, and John Miur led to one of the greatest creations of our government as Yosemite became a National Park.

Pedaling up Rt 120 Tioga Road in Yosemite NP

President Teddy Roosevelt expanded Yosemite and public land protections "for the benefit and enjoyment of the people." when he signed the Antiquities Act in 1906 after an inspiring 3-day camping trip with John Miur. That year only 5,500 people visited Yosemite, compared to the nearly 2.3 million visitors that 1974 Bob and I were part of – far less than the peak in 2016 of 5.03 million visitors. *"And still they lead me back to the long and winding road."* [6] Depending on the year,

25-44 percent of visitors are "lead back" by the long road to Yosemite for a return visit. Unfortunately, what was once free for us touring bicyclists in 1974 now incurs a $20.00 entrance fee and a pre-paid reservation in 2024.

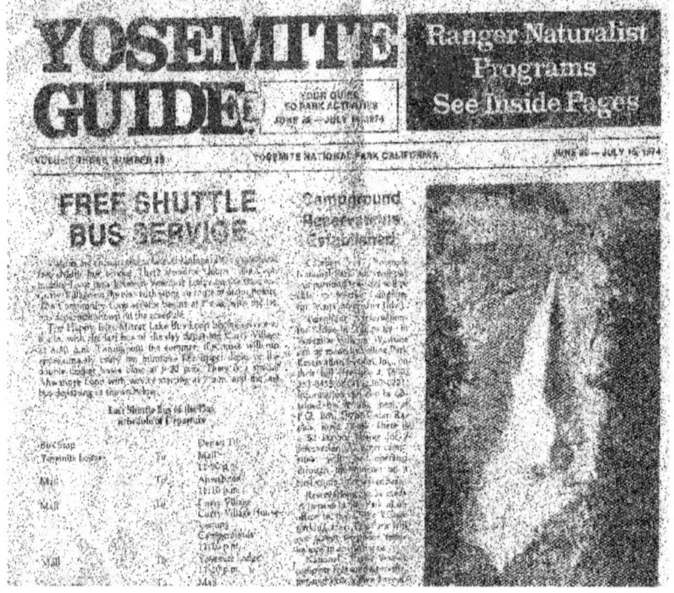

YOSEMITE GUIDE

YOUR GUIDE TO PARK ACTIVITIES JUNE 26 — JULY 16, 1974

Ranger Naturalist Programs See Inside Pages

YOSEMITE NATIONAL PARK CALIFORNIA

JUNE 26 — JULY 16, 1974

FREE SHUTTLE BUS SERVICE

Campground Reservations Established

"The wild and windy night, that the rain washed away, has left a pool of tears, crying for the day." [6] First came the cottony cumulus clouds with their ominous black underbellies, then the distant sound of thunder, followed by the first giant drops of rain. We inhaled the smell of rain striking hot pavement that is recognized

by road cyclists as well as children playing in the street as they run for shelter from the rain. Australian scientists named this "petrichor" in 1964, a name that is far more forgettable than this uniquely memorable scent. Petrichor is composed of a blend of ozone (created by lightning striking molecules of oxygen and nitrogen), geosmin (a compound created by soil bacteria that is released into the air by striking raindrops), and volatile plant oils captured in the soil and on the road. These raindrops were certainly refreshing at first but would soon turn frigid.

In the pouring rain we slogged up another 2,400 feet of elevation gain to Crane Flats where we entered the upper montane forest. Pure stands of red fir and sections of road lined with lodgepole pine could not shield us from the cold rain and mist that shrouded the mountains. After a soaking night in wet sleeping bags, we painstakingly pedaled up another 3,500 feet of elevation through the green and granite landscape which finally led to the subalpine forest of Tuolome

Meadows. The rain stopped for a while, enabling the fragrance of wildflowers to be released before night fell on our final night in Yosemite. We awoke to glistening ice crystals on our moist tent ceiling but were welcomely warmed by the radiant heat arising from the asphalt as we descended from Tioga Pass into the sunny dry high desert. *"Well, the rain exploded with a mighty crash, as we fell into the sun, and the first one said to the second one there 'I hope you're having fun.'"*[7] Boy, were we!

How different parts of these magnificent forests would look after the ravages of the Bark Beetles decades after the recording demise of the British Beatle. By 2016 the US Forest Service reported over 102 million dead trees in California due to beetle kill, and 2.4 million were in Yosemite National Park alone. There are many species of bark beetles, each with its own preferred species of tree bark to munch on. Like college spring breakers in cheap Florida hotels, bark beetle sex drive is apparently stimulated by warmer temperatures. Yosemite has been warming at a rate of 3.4°F per century compared to the pre-2016 rate of 1.6°F per century. Sequential years of drought, low snowpack, and decades of fire mitigation without forest thinning have created ideal conditions for these destructive insects.

The adult has a hard black outer shell covering its minute ¼ inch long body. Emerging from the bark each spring, the mature beetle briefly lives outside of the tree. After locating the closest tasty Ponderosa or Lodgepole pine (the bigger the trunk the better) they initiate their "attack" by boring into the bark, under which most of their lifecycle is spent. They will secrete pheromones that attract mates, and any nearby adults to swarm to their tree. The happy couples then produce eggs inside intricate bark tunnels called galleries. Eggs then evolve into larvae who eat away at the Cambian bark layer choking off the tree's nutrient supply. Bark Beetles additionally bring along a fungus that destroys the tree's ability to secrete sap. In a low infestation year pines increase their sap flow to thwart the beetle invasion, but the disabling of this defense system and the destruction of the Cambian layer can kill a massive pine in just a few weeks.

Initially the pine needles turn a reddish brown and within a year the tree is a standing corpse. Depending on the diversity of pine species, the forest view could be marred by conspicuous isolated tall dead trees, or in the case of homogenous beetle-prone forest tracts, large swaths of brown and gray lifeless pines scar the landscape. The bark beetles were certainly present in the pines we pedaled past in 1974, but never in these numbers or in forests so environmentally stressed.

Fortunately for us, all these same forests in 2024 appear to have survived several bark beetle epidemics and are slowly regenerating with naturally beetle-resistant species of conifers. Loss of the preferred ponderosa and lodgepole pines to years of beetles feasting on them have eliminated the cheap Florida hotels for these spring breakers. Improvement in drought conditions, some colder winters, aggressive removal of beetle killed tress, and controlled burns to keep forests thinner have all contributed to forest recovery. Forests have changed in the past 50 years. Yet the elimination of the Bark Beetle from western US forests remains as impossible in 2024 as a Beatles reunion was in 1974.

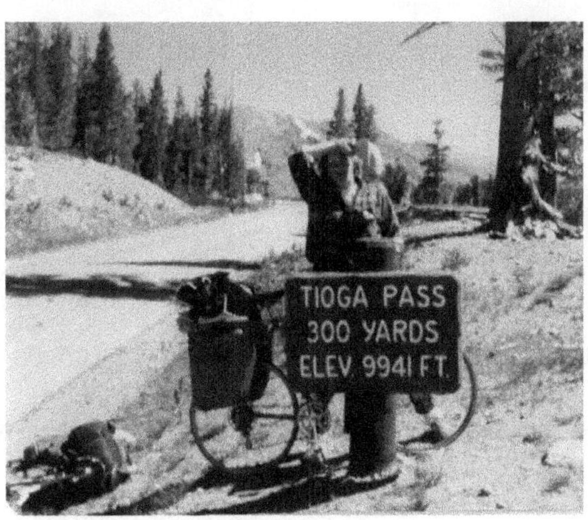

KC at Tioga Pass in Yosemite National Park

The southeastern side of Tioga Pass treated us to a 14-mile downhill. I never even moved my pedals for 10 miles of the plunge onto the high desert road leading to Benton Hot Springs. We stopped at a laundromat in Le Vining, California and washed all our belongings. By 3:00 pm we hit the long desert road and by 4:00 pm Bob had two tire blowouts and was out of water. We crossed a small clear water stream and soaked our feet in it. Bob took a chance and filled his water bottle there. Anxious to get off the road, Bob raced ahead and arrived at Benton Hot Springs one hour and one beer ahead of me.

This two-building town served us the best tasting Coors beer I have ever had to this day, and an invitation to enjoy the owner's private hot spring. Steaming water gushed up from the rocky bottom of a 6 x 6-foot concrete tank that overflowed into a tree lined pond. We soaked away two days' worth of aches and road grime and got out before our legs were too weak and rubbery to lumber into the town of Benton – our last stop in California.

Day 9 and we finally entered Nevada where their welcoming road sign declared "Recreation Unlimited". Route 6 then rose from 5,600 ft to the 7,167 ft Montgomery Pass where we found the air-conditioned "Casino" – which claimed to be the world's highest elevation casino. I plopped 25 cents (1/12 of my daily budget) into a slot machine which came up a losing "7-cherry-$". Unfortunately, Mongomery Pass is now a ghost town as the Casino burnt down in 2011 and was never rebuilt.

We did, however, devise a winning strategy to cross the desert into Tonopah, Nevada. By stopping every 5 miles or 30 minutes (whichever came first) we would stop for a brief rest, a handful of Gorp and some water. We made it to Coaldale, NV where we waited out the midday heat at a truck stop eating their Friday Frank and Potato Salad special with a side of 20 glasses of water. The main building was formerly a part of the hospital in Tonopah which was purchased by Eldon Parson in the 1940s and trucked 40 miles up to Coaldale.

Regrettably the gas pumps were closed by the EPA in 1993 due to leaking fuel tanks and the restaurant burned to the ground in 2006. Coaldale is now another ghost town, but in its prime I was able to do some journal writing and unstitch, patch and restitch two flattened sew up tires.

Our first slot machine in Casino at Mongomery Pass, Nevada

With the wind at our backs, we made it to the outskirts of Tonopah, Nevada and slept at a roadside rest. We ate our emergency freeze dried meals as we were too exhausted to pedal into town and get groceries.The next morning disaster struck.

Chapter 7

Trapped in Tonopah

Day 10 July 13

Tonopah, Nevada to Tonopah, Nevada: 0 miles

It sounded simple enough in Tom Cuthbertson's Anybody's Bike Book section on Rules of Thumb.

> "#6. Keep all bearings adjusted properly. Your bicycle has between 150 and 200 ball bearings. To keep them all rolling smoothly, you have to learn to adjust the cups and cones in which they run."

Tired of listening to the grinding and clunking

coming from my freewheel, I sat on the curb of the dusty street in front of the hardware store in Tonopah, Nevada and removed my rear wheel. I started to carefully remove the two pin-holed inner cover and take apart the 5 sprocket freewheel which promptly seemed to come apart like slices of bread flaking off a loaf. With this, of course, the 40 small ball bearings tumbled into the sand-filled street gutter which appeared to have been last swept in 1874. With no bike shop or purveyor of small ball bearings in this town of just under 2,000 souls we turned for advice from the Mizpah Hotel, which also housed a restaurant and casino and served as a bus stop for coaches serving the Las Vegas-Tonopah-Reno route. In a place labeled in 1975 as "Tonopah Today: The town that wouldn't die", there was no hesitation on how to solve my bike part dilemma.

"Why don't you just look in that phone book there and find a bike shop in Reno. It's only about 300 miles away. Maybe they can send you the parts you need by bus. It comes through town twice a day. Next one arrives at 1:30 am tonight," declared the heavily perfumed front desk lady.

So, I cold-called a bicycle shop in Reno, from Tonopah, and told the unbelievably benevolent shopkeeper my story.

"Yeah sure, we stock that freewheel and I have plenty of those ball bearings. Will you be coming here to pick them up?"

"Well, not exactly. The front desk at the Mizpah Hotel says that a bus stops here twice a day, and maybe you could send the ball bearings with the bus driver." I held my breath in anticipation of his reply.

"Yeah sure. The bus stops right up the street from here and I can do that."

"So how much do I owe you, and how shall I pay you and the bus driver?" I assumed this would really blow my $3/day budget.

"Yeah, don't worry about that. I can send my bill to your home in West Virginia.".

Brilliant! No Amazon, UPS or FedEx – no PayPal or Venmo - no problem! Although UPS started delivering packages in 1907 in Seattle, Washington, they did not clear the necessary regulatory requirements to operate in Nevada until 1975, making it the first package delivery company to theoretically serve every address in the US. FedEx had started delivering packages via 14 aircraft out of Memphis, Tennessee, in 1973, but Tonopah, Nevada was certainly not one of the 25 cities that were served. Lucky for us that Greyhound bus was still in the package delivery business, as they ceased this service in 2022.

This silver mining town with its boom-and-bust history is situated halfway between Las Vegas and Reno. We were indeed in the Twilight Zone of the "middle of nowhere", and simultaneously (as their tourist motto says), in the "middle of everywhere".

Downtown Tonopah at the foot of Mount Butler

So, it was here in Tonopah that we were trapped - waiting for a bus hundreds of miles away, to deliver precious freewheel ball bearings, promised by a guy I never met, before he was even paid. What could go wrong with that? At least we would have the first day in nearly 2 weeks that we would not be riding our bikes.

Unfortunately, in 1974 Tonopah was a shadow of its peak population of nearly 20,000, pulling millions of dollars' worth of silver and gold from the ground in the early 1900's. With no more mining, the railroads had all shut down since 1947. With no major industry for employment, Tonopah -like so many small western mining towns – set out to revitalize their economy with tourism. They were not very far along that path in 1974.

The Tonopah Historic Mining Park, and the Tonopah Stargazing Park (Tonopah is one of darkest places in the US) would take decades to launch. The town would have to wait until 1985 for Clarence David's children Leona & Leroy to open the Clown Motel next to the Cemetery where their beloved father was buried. They bizarrely displayed all 150 of their father's clown collection in the hotel that would be dubbed "America's Scariest Hotel "and become a bucket list site for ghost hunters and paranormal investigators. The Cline family would purchase the boarded up Mizpah Hotel in 2011 to restore it and the town to their "Queen of the Silver Camps" status. Slowly but surely Tonopah has become a tourist destination in 2024.

Other projects were not as successful. The infamous Tonopah Test Range started design and eventual testing of the F-117 Blackhawk stealth fighter in the 1970s, but nuclear and chemical weapon testing contaminated much of the site which has remained largely dormant since 2008. Even Tonopah's promising 2014 Crescent Energy Solar Project using molten sodium as a heat transfer medium for solar energy storage has been intermittently offline since 2016. With ongoing technical and financial complications, it has yet to produce the originally expected megawatts of energy.

But hey, Tonopah had a community park and swimming pool with a 75-cent admission fee in 1974, and that's where we hung out with the locals during our waiting day. We were invited to play basketball by a middle-aged guy named Tony and three of his cousins. At the pool park we cooked ground beef with the new processed food sensation Hamburger Helper, along with a big can of beans. The saddest thing is that nobody (including us) thought that this was weird or disgusting. We were invited to join an evening pool party which ended up being a large number of underage youths drinking beer and tequila. Feeling more like chaperones than drinking buddies, we left the party at 10:00 pm.

There was one lonely worn wooden bench in front of the Mizpah Hotel that served as the bus waiting room. We watched drunks stagger in and out of the casino/bar and tried sleeping upright on that bench until 1:30 am – the scheduled Reno bus arrival time. A particularly inebriated gentleman shared a long-winded account of Tonopah's glory days, and eventually got around to asking why we were wearing bicycle clothing in the middle of the night. As if struck with a lightning bolt of sobriety, he suddenly relayed that he heard an overhead announcement that the bus from Reno was delayed and would not arrive until 4:10 am. It was time for another strategy. We took turns going inside the hotel restaurant, where the announcement was verified, and were repeatedly given a menu and ice water by the understanding waitress even though we never ordered anything.

"I don't know how much longer we can keep wasting this poor waitress's time like this," said Bob. "See that dozer over there? I'm gonna go check out that big blade. It looks like a person could just about fit in there."

I followed him out of the building and paused at the entryway. The next thing I saw was him scampering across the streetlight lit avenue and hopping into the cradling front bucket of the bulldozer. Bob's head popped up and he yelled back to me.

"Goodnight! Wake me up when the bus comes."

We alternated hourly sleeping in the surprisingly comfortable shovel of that parked bulldozer – demolisher of buildings by day – bike hobo hotel by night. Mercifully, the bus arrived at 4:10 am and the driver clad in his official blue jacket and black billed uniform hat with the wavy blue and red Greyhound badge opened the door. Diesel fumes never smelt so good.

"Are you the guys expecting a package from Reno?" he shouted over the bus engine.

"Yes sir!" I replied while having a strange urge to salute him.

With that he handed me an envelope containing my name and over 50 perfectly new freewheel ball bearings.

"How much do I owe you, sir?" I asked.

"Nothing son. The bike shop took care of that."

We ecstatically tore open the envelope, greased the bearings and carefully placed them in my freewheel. The sun was just starting to rise when we finished, so we loaded up and sped out of Tonopah. We made haste in the 100-degree heat toward our previously planned destination of Warm Springs, Nevada.

The Reno bike shop never did send me a bill.

Chapter 8

Nye, it was a stampede!

Day 11 July 14

Tonopah, Nevada to Warm Springs, Nevada: 50 miles

Day 12 July 15

Warm Spgs, NV to Ash Springs,NV:104 miles (20 by jeep)

"What the heck!" exclaimed Bob.

"Wild horses!" I shouted as we squeezed our brakes and slowed to see several muscular horses with matted manes and tails gallop across Rt 6.

I guess I knew they existed, but in 1974 I was more familiar with the chorus of the Rolling Stones *Wild*

Horses[8]. Of course, 50 years later I best recall the beautiful rendition by Britain's Got Talent singing savant Susan Boyle.[9] *"Wild horses couldn't drag me away…Wild, wild horses, we'll ride them some day."*

Thought to have descended from the Spanish horses and burros (aka donkeys) that Cortez brought to Mexico in 1519, these diverse herds were estimated to number over 2 million in 1900. Public outcry and concern over their welfare and diminished numbers prompted passage of the 1971 Wild Horse and Burro Act.

> "Congress finds and declares that wild free-roaming horses and burros are living symbols of the historic and pioneer spirit of the West; that they contribute to the diversity of life forms within the Nation and enrich the lives of the American people; and that these horses and burros are fast disappearing from the American scene. It is the policy of Congress that wild free-roaming horses and burros shall be protected from capture, branding, harassment, or death; and to accomplish this they are to be considered in the area where presently found, as an integral part of the natural system of the public lands."

The fatal flaw for horses was the fine print stipulation that the herds be managed to their 1971 numbers of 17,000 – a number that was seriously flawed and well below the Bureau of Land Management's actual horse count in 1974 of 42,000.

The decline from 2 million to less than 50,000 was largely due to the myth that wild horses encroached on successful cattle and sheep herd grazing. Hunting wild horses was permitted, and their grazing areas were reduced by barbed wire fencing of bargain-leased public lands by ranchers. Wild horses were left the barren water-poor lands of little agricultural value. The poor feral burros competed with big horn sheep, so western wildlife agencies allegedly wanted them removed so that game animals could flourish and create the downstream revenue produced by hunting licenses and taxed ammo and gun sales.

Despite the 1971 law, still in 1974, there were reports of mustang hunting licenses being issued. Wild horses were run down to deathly exhaustion by aircraft and snowmobiles, herded off cliffs, shot when corralled and buried in mass graves or rendered for dog food. As a Nevada rancher was quoted in the April 22, 1974, issue of Newsweek, "if the bureau would just look the other way for two weeks, we could make this cattle country again." Brutal treatment indeed for these amazingly adapted animals that can withstand summer heat and freezing winters, endure 2 days without water and can range 10-15 miles away from water sources.

"We saw some wild horses on Rt 6 today", I told the Warm Springs, Nevada, bartender, trying to make some small talk.

"Yeah, shit, there are thousands of them here in Nye County.", he mumbled while wiping the bar.

There was no hint of fondness for them in his voice, and I suspect he did not buy into the notion that they "enrich the lives of the American people." We were in the middle of the three county Nevada Wild Horse Range, in the state which still in 2024 debatably holds more of America's wild horses than any other state. In a far too common contradictory legal environment, the range lies within the Nellis Range Complex where the Air Force does weapon testing and flight training. Yet despite a wild horse range designation as "principally" for wild horses, the BLM says that wild horse use is secondary to military use on this land. No cattle grazing or burros are supposed to be there. Little comfort for the 71 wild horses who died in 2007 from nitrate poisoning on the Tonopah Test Range, a test site on the edge of the Nellis Range.

Allegedly the BLM has been overestimating the number of wild horses to legitimize removal/disposal of "excess horses" by orders of magnitude. By 1992 the Nevada wild horse population was estimated to be 33,434 by the BLM. Michael Blake, the author of Dances with Wolves, helped fund a private survey by horse advocates that logged over 250 hours counting Nevada's wild horses from airplanes, and they found only 8,300 live horses – about one-fourth of the federal estimate. The BLM countered that they used more accurate helicopter flights to do their count and spent $300,000 compared to only $42,000 by the citizen group who used airplanes.

Now don't get me wrong, I do respect many aspects of the BLM mission and accomplishments. My favorite ex-son-in-law Cody is a BLM law enforcement officer who along with one other officer patrols and protects 1 million acres of BLM land near Moab, Utah. Their rescue of lost or injured desert adventurers, and apprehension of persons engaged in a host of criminal activities on our remote public lands is truly admirable, and terribly under-appreciated. The BLM did start their adoption program where for as little as a $125 application fee one can adopt a wild horse or burro that has been rounded up to reduce the "Animal Unit Months" or AUM on federal land. You can then receive a $1,000 incentive after you successfully care for them for one year. In fact, almost 300,000 animals have been adopted out since 1971, saving them from slaughter (very unpopular to the public) or the limbo of life in a

BLM maintained holding facility (at a cost of millions to the US taxpayer).

Sadly, in 2024 only 800 wild horses are reported to remain in Nevada according to the American Wild Horse organization. They report that the BLM has a plan to reduce this to 300-500 horses and remove all burros over the next 10 years. A far cry from the 1974 "thousands" of wild horses reported to live in Ny county by the bartender of Warm Springs.

The same barkeep enthusiastically replied "I don't give a shit" when asked if it was OK to pitch our tent for the night near the picnic table beside his establishment. We quickly erected our tent and promptly conked out.

"What is that?" I thought in my half-awakened state as I felt and heard the ground rumble.

"What the heck?", exclaimed Bob.

As the noise became louder the ground and tent

walls shook. I peeked out between the flaps into the dusty moonlit darkness to see what seemed like the hooves, shanks and fetlocks of every wild horse in Nye County. This wasn't an earthquake – it was a Nye wild horse stampede!

I'm pretty sure we assumed the fetal position in preparation for death by hooves. It seemed to last for minutes but was probably only a few seconds. When the thunderous noise abated and the dust started to clear we emerged from our tent expecting to find our bikes, and our gear flattened and mangled. Incredibly to me (as our only horsemanship was sitting on a slow rope led pony at Oglebay Park), our bikes and packs were untouched and not a single tent stake or guy rope was disturbed.

As we later recounted this story to actual equestrian people, they assured us that horses instinctually circumvent stepping on things to avoid tripping and injuring their legs. Nonetheless, I credited our survival to the Wild Horse spirit god of Nevada as I caught a glimpse of 10 horses galloping across the road and off into the sagebrush and juniper. I guess the other 1,000 must have run far ahead of them?

We were unable to get any real sleep after that and fearing another stampede and what looked like 75 miles of waterless desert road between Diablo and Ash Springs, we packed up and pedaled into the darkness of the pre-dawn hours. Bob wasn't too thrilled about me pushing for the whole riding in the dark idea, and things got a bit tense. It began to rain, and Bob's freewheel jammed at Diablo, Nevada. The only structure in this devilish 'town' was a road maintenance building. The worker there refused to lend us the use of some tools ("State property, boys"). We pitched our tent and slept until 10:00 am in the rain, hoping for a better day when we woke up. By then the maintenance gate was padlocked, no vehicles had passed us all night or morning, and we decided that I would pedal on for help while Bob would try and hitch a ride if any vehicles appeared.

After pedaling 40 miles past Diablo, Bob pulled up alongside me hanging out of the camper passenger window with a beer in his hand and a smile on his face. This elderly couple had to have been the only vehicle driving on what their tour book said was "Nevada's hottest and most desolate desert". They stopped and fixed me a sandwich and beer lunch and replenished my dwindling water supply. We were almost to Ash Springs, and I decided to pedal on while Bob rode ahead with them in search of tools to fix his bike. I was feeling relieved that we had a plan to meet at Ash Springs as I pedaled along the flat windless road.

Calamity was following us that day – and finally caught up. Suddenly my rear tire blew out and I could not inflate my spare as I had bent my pump somewhere in Yosemite. So out went my thumb and within one minute out of the shimmering road mirage came what had to be only the second vehicle on Rt 375 that day.

Fred, a silver miner, pulled over in his Jeep Wagoneer and offered me a ride. He schooled me in the business of silver mining, federal mining laws, and the transformation of the desert in rain. He dropped me off at the Ash Springs Hot Springs – a lush green desert oasis where we camped and swam in the glorious warm pond waters.

Our tent pitched at Ash Springs, Nevada

The desert and nature can be dangerous and brutal. We were lucky in so many ways that day.

We needed a lot more in the coming weeks.

Chapter 9

Dam Luck and a Crash in Santa Claus

Day 13 July 16

Warm Spgs, NV to Hoover Dam, AZ: 140 miles (100 by pickup)

Day 14 July 17

Hoover Dam, Arizona to Kingman, Arizona: 84 miles

Day 15 July 18

Kingman, Arizona to Seligman, Arizona: 80 miles

Day 16 July 19

Seligman, AZ to Grand Canyon, AZ: 104 miles (40 by pickup)

Biology and ecology taught me that water could both sustain life and end life. On day 13 we took a last swim in the natural hot springs pool in Ash Springs before heading out to Hoover Dam. Fortunately, we never became ill after these impromptu swims in nature's hot tubs. Sadly, the pristine spring we relished in 1974 is closed in 2024. Besides some structural wall hazards, it is now a known habitat for *Naegleria fowleri*. a parasite that naturally occurs in warm and hot freshwaters feeding on bacteria. I had not come across that germ yet after 3 years as a biology major. Tragically, two-year-old Woodrow Bundy inhaled some water containing *Naegleria fowleri* while splashing in Ash Springs in July of 2023 and died 7 days later. This brain eating amoeba can enter the nose of humans to then travel up the olfactory nerves to the brain causing headache, fever, seizures, coma and death.

The Centers for Disease Control reports that only four people (3%) have survived out of 157 known infected individuals in the United States from 1962 to 2022. I never saw this infection in my 45-year medical career, but I performed spinal taps on patients with high fever, headache and altered consciousness. I rarely had to insert that long skinny needle into the fluid filled sac that surrounds the lower spine of a person who had been recently swimming in a pond or lake. When I did, the buried memory of *Naegleria fowleri* would emerge, as do many rare diagnoses in the minds of physicians when we don't know what's wrong with our patients. Thankfully there is a cocktail of new antibiotics in 2024 that can cure this infection if promptly diagnosed.

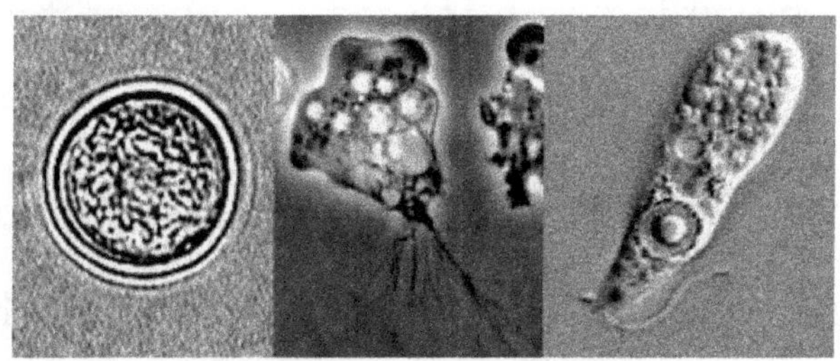

Naegleria fowleri *Life Cycle: Environmental Cyst* (Left)*, Infective Amoeba stage* (Center)*, Flagella (tail) stage* (Right*)*

The best prevention is to keep your head above water when swimming in warm ponds and hot natural springs. Indeed, what was true in 1974 is still true 50 years later - the known risks we expose ourselves to in life are far outnumbered by those that we are unaware of.

The combination grocery store-campground-gas station that ran our Ash Springs oasis was managed by a brother and sister cowboy duo who also owned two ranches. They even drove the cattle 100 miles north to their winter pasture via horseback. The brother had a dental appointment in Las Vegas the next day and we joined him for the 100-mile ride across more Nevada desert. He passionately spoke of the wildflowers that would be blooming with the recent rain and the plant and animal life that abounds in his desert. I was spellbound by his conversation and asked a hundred questions, while Bob (the accountant major) could only muster an occasional polite "Wow, that's interesting" comment. The biology and botany nerdfest ended at an amazing bike shop in Las Vegas where we were offered free access to the tools needed to repair Bob's bike. Then we navigated the Vegas traffic and made it to our Hoover Dam destination by afternoon.

At 726 feet tall, it was by far the largest dam that I had ever seen. Cycling across the 45-foot wide top of the dam can no longer be easily replicated as an adjacent 4-lane bridge was built to remove dam traffic and increase dam security. A limited number of vehicles are still allowed to slowly drive over the dam after going through a security checkpoint. Opened in 2010, the Mike Callaghan-Pat Tillman Memorial Bridge is the widest concrete arch bridge in the Western Hemisphere and at 890 feet above the Colorado River, the second highest bridge in the US. Fortunately, despite being only 30 miles from Las Vegas where fortunes are regularly lost, very few people have committed suicide by jumping off the bridge or the dam.

Hoover Dam was constructed during the Great Depression, attracting workers from around the country to seek the new and promising job opportunity to work for an average wage of 62.5 cents an hour or $1,825 a year (by comparison the Congressmen who approved the dam project made $8,663, doctors $3,382 and coal miners $723 annually).

KC at Hoover Dam

The purpose was to control flooding, improve navigation, produce energy, and provide water storage for agricultural and potable water for downstream areas like California and Arizona. Decades of battles over water in the American West preceded the 1922 Colorado River Compact and Boulder Canyon Project Act. The famous Colorado river explorer John Wesley Powell warned in 1893 that we were "piling up a heritage of conflict and litigation over water rights, for there is not sufficient water to supply these lands!"

Fifty -two years before our cross country journey the Colorado river water rights were allocated to seven states, including California and Wyoming across which the river does not flow. The water rights were calculated in million acre-feet annually (1 acre-foot of water is enough to cover one acre of land with 1 foot of water, about 326,000 gallons). Unfortunately, the founding assumption of an average annual water flow of 17.3 million acre-feet (maf) was an overestimation. For example, the flow was only about 5.5 maf in 1974.

Now 50 years later the Lake Mead we viewed from Hoover Dam is scarred with a "bathtub ring" of calcium carbonate over 150 feet tall. The water reservoir now holds less than half of the amount it was designed to store. The federal government is even paying California's Imperial Irrigation District $77.6 million to not take 100,000 acre-feet of water from Lake Mead in

2024. The National Park Service warns that the current water level of 1,060 feet elevation is dangerously close to the minimum level at 950 feet needed to run the hydroelectric turbines at Hoover Dam. In 2024 water rights lawyers and lobbyists scramble for judgements and legislation to keep more water in Lake Mead.

It would take us another 264 road miles before we could see the Colorado River again at the Grand Canyon, but at the top of the hill on the Arizona side of the Hoover Dam we experienced something almost as wondrous. An older couple driving their tow behind camper had seen us biking up the steep grade and waved us over to a surprise sit down lunch of pop, water, and sandwiches they had prepared for us at the roadside rest. Checkered tablecloth, paper napkins, that soft white Wonder Bread, crisp lettuce, tangy French's mustard, and that bitter, yet sweet, sausage taste of Oscar Myer bologna were nearly gourmet to road hungry me in 1974 - not so much in 2024. We camped near the couple, Nora and Bob, and then ate breakfast together in the warm soft morning desert wind. We wished them a happy 31st anniversary as we started off on Day 14. I have always wanted to do something like Nora and Bob's act of kindness now that I am retired but have not yet been in a similar situation. Peg and I might have to rent a camper on our 31st anniversary in 2029 and check out the Hoover Dam.

We posed for goofy photos near large desert yuccas and visited rock shops as we pedaled through the much greener desert of Arizona. We waited out a brief rain in a bar at Grasshopper, Arizona (population 5) which likely contributed to Bob crashing outside of Santa Claus, Arizona (although he didn't think so). Santa Claus was not the happy place that its name suggested. The heyday of the Christmas Tree Inn and Cinderella's Doll House were long gone. Only one of the few wooden buildings was still in use as a gift shop and post office when we passed by. There was a time that you could send them your addressed Christmas cards and for an extra twenty-five cents of postage get them postmarked in Santa Clause, Arizona. Sadly, the town and post office closed in 1995, and the remaining abandoned buildings were demolished in 2021.

KC pointing west past desert yuccas

Bob was drafting me and didn't see me slow down to scratch an itch (or perhaps the beer in Grasshopper contributed to me not announcing that I was slowing down). We touched tires and he immediately hit the pavement resulting in a severely bent front derailleur and a scratched elbow. Unable to repair it, he was left with a 5-speed and no bike shop likely for many miles.

"KC ! Why did you slow down?" yelled Bob while lying on the roadside.

"Sorry Bob, Are you alright?" I asked.

"Yea if you consider a bleeding elbow and a bent front derailleur – alright," he replied.

"I didn't know you were riding up my butt," I apologetically replied.

"We were drafting! What did you expect," muttered Bob.

He wasn't one to get all mad and demonstrative. I suspected that he blamed me for the accident, and I guess I was – partly. My discovery that I had somehow lost the first aid kit did not help the situation.

We didn't speak a lot for the next 24 hours as the

miles went by slowly through Hualapai reservation where poverty and boredom seemed everywhere. A cold evening rain and headwinds forced us to break our budget on a $4.00 KOA campsite with a hot shower and a dry sheltered dining area.

We were 'all good' by the next day – the silent drama-less way most guys seem to resolve minor differences. We mutually decided to forego another State Police incident as our road merged to share a 40-mile stretch of interstate highway with a large "No Bicycles" sign. Instead, we hitched a ride to Williams and pedaled the remaining 64 miles to the Grand Canyon. Along our route we were joined by Willie, a 20-something army vet majoring in drama at the University of Arizona who rode along with us almost all the way to the Canyon. He carried an impressive array of tools and was able to fix Bob's derailleur as we waited out another rainstorm in a roadside bathroom. Frustrated with the rain, Willie peeled off at the Grand Canyon Airport exit to seek shelter. Bob and I pushed on to the South Rim Grand Canyon Village n the first rain that the area had seen since New Year's Day.

The rain turned to cold hail as we pulled into Mather Campground.

"We'd like a campsite for the night," I shouted over the noise of ice pellets striking the entrance kiosk roof.

The chubby mustached ranger replied, "Sorry boys, but the campground is FULL." His mustache twitched and I began to shiver.

Chapter 10

More Water Rights & Wrongs and a Desert Warning

Day 17 July 20

Grand Canyon, Arizona to Cameron, Arizona: 57 miles

A guy named Ed from Ohio overheard the Ranger speaking with us and offered to have us pitch our tent on his RV site for free. A hot shower and warm meal saved the day. After a great night's sleep under clearing skies, it was time to explore. It is difficult to describe the Grand Canyon better than John Muir.

"The Grand Cañon of the Colorado will seem as novel to you, as unearthly in the color and grandeur and quantity of its architecture, as if you had found it after death, on some other star; so incomparably lovely and grand and supreme it is above all other cañons."[10]

I stood at the Canyon rim and stared in awe at the vast mesmerizing vista. It was like standing at the ocean's edge with that same primordial need to take it all in. One of those rare places where you feel like a speck in the universe. Where I wondered how I could or would make a difference in this huge world of ours.

Through the coin operated view machines mounted at the South Rim we peered deep into the Canyon floor. We saw the ribbon of river far below and occasional stripes of white water between long quietly flowing pools and small sandy beaches. Fifty years later you can purchase a ticket for $51 to walk out on a glass cantilever sky bridge extending 70 feet out over,

and 4,000 feet above the Canyon floor. The river is a clearer green now compared to the muddy brown we saw in 1974, and the riverbanks are also greener due to the upstream effects of Lake Powell and its controversial Glen Canyon Dam. A closer look in 2024 led me to understand why water rights attorney and judge John E. Thorson said, "Water links us to our neighbor in a way more profound and complex than any other."

In the 1950s the Upper Basin states of Colorado,

Wyoming, and Utah felt a need for their own reservoir. It basically would ensure capacity to deliver the stipulated 7.5 maf water flow to the Lower Basin states during times of drought without having to cut back on Upper Basin consumption. After all, the Colorado River has its origins in the mountains of Wyoming and Colorado.

The very remote Glen Canyon had no national parks or major cities and was selected for a dam despite vigorous opposition from environmental groups. Groups like the Sierra Club foresaw destruction of riparian environments, removal of silt, and dropping of the water temperature downstream of the dam. The Navajo tribe opposed the dam for its forced relocation of Native inhabitants, flooding of ancestral lands and infringement on the sacred Rainbow Bridge where Blessing Way ceremonies and other rituals had been performed for ages. When we pedaled through the Colorado Basin in 1974 the Glen Canyon Dam was just 8 years old and would not fill Lake Powell until 1980.

Also, in 1974 several Navajo medicine men filed suit against the Secretary of the Interior, the Commissioner of the Bureau of Reclamation, and the Director of the National Park Service on the grounds that the dam and lake denied their rights to conduct religious ceremonies and had adversely affected the Navajo life and culture through its environmental impact. The court concluded that the economic interests of the government outweighed the Navajo religious interests – even though Lake Powel is on Navajo Nation reservation land. This traditional location is now accessed by a 14-mile trail or by boat (available for $147 for a paid tour, or via private watercraft), and gets 200,000 visitors annually.

Many still consider the Glen Canyon Dam and Lake Powell to be one of the largest environmental disasters in America. The dam collects silt that formed and replenished the sandy beaches along the Grand Canyon of the Colorado river. The silt also scrubbed the walls of Grand Canyon during yearly floods (now limited by dam control), which kept the narrow banks free from choking vegetation. Now the invasive tamarisk or salt cedar is the dominant plant with an ability to suck water springs dry and secrete salts that inhibit other native plant growth. The clear cold water that flows from the bottom of Lake Powell into the Grand Canyon has altered the fish ecosystem as well.

Economically, the Glen Canyon Dam has declining hydroelectricity production due to the dramatic drop in water level since 2000. When optimally filled, the Lake Powell water level is at an elevation of 3,700 feet. In April 2024 the level was 3,558 feet elevation – just 68 feet above lowest level needed for the turbines to operate. If it drops another 120 feet below that, "dead pool status" occurs – the inability to allow water to pass downstream from the Glenn Canyon Dam.

In 2024 there are proposals to allow Lake Powell to dry up so that Lake Mead can survive. Allowing the

Colorado river to resume its previous free flow through the Glen Canyon would be accomplished by ceasing hydroelectricity production and by passing the Glen Canyon Dam. One million gallons of water are lost annually to evaporation over the 180-mile-long lake surface area, as well as loss through the porous sandstone side walls of Lake Powell.

Environment groups like Living Rivers and the Glen Canyon Institute point towards a "One Dam" (ie. The Hoover Dam) solution, also called the "Lake Mead First" solution. Even the Abatti brothers who own the largest water consuming agriculture lands in the Imperial Valley of California admit that there just is not enough water to keep two giant reservoirs operational. The Upper Basin states are pushing for a mandatory reduction in the flow allocation to the Lower Basin States, and the 30 Native American tribes who are collectively in possession of up to 25% of the Colorado river rights demand that they be at the negotiation tables this time around.

Our final look at this awesome spectacle of nature ended at Desert View Watchtower. Ater twenty miles in the flat high desert, we then coasted for 10 miles of fantastic downhill along the Little Colorado River and arrived in Cameron, Arizona, at 5:00 pm. It looked more like an Indian settlement, and it frankly took some getting used to being a minority among so many Native Americans.

"Where did you boys ride those bicycles from?" asked the Navajo waitress at the Cameron Trading Post's Grand Canyon Restaurant. Her black hair, round face and slight smile framed her friendly eyes. She reminds me now of the incredible Navajo medical assistant I had in my final years of practicing medicine.

"Well, we started in San Francisco and are headed to the Atlantic Ocean, "I replied, "but we missed the post office hours. We had friends and family send us letters and some cookies and have been thinking about them the whole ride in from the Grand

Canyon.”

“Don’t worry. The Post Office lady likes to take a jeep ride at the end of her day. She’ll be back in an hour or so and will probably let you guys get your mail”, she very matter of fact replied as if federal Post Office business hours didn’t really matter here.

So, we waited and entertained some Navajo children curious about our bikes and packs. Eventually, a wiry white woman with gray hair pulled up in her dusty 4-wheeler. After introducing ourselves she immediately recalled our general delivery mail and kindly retrieved our letters and packages. We shared our candy with the Navajo kids, and after locking up the Post Office, the postmistress joined us.

"So where are you guys headed next?" she asked.

“We’re headed for Durango, Colorado”, I offered.

“Well, that’s a long way across some pretty hot

isolated territory. I hope you have sturdy bikes and can carry a lot of water", she said looking over her horned rim eyeglasses.

It was a warning we would take seriously.

Chapter 11

Trust and Risk

Day 18 July 21

Cameron, AZ to Durango, Colorado: 250 miles (by hippie van)

Day 18 began with a trust/risk analysis. I was comfortable with the trust associated with speeding downhill. Like all cyclists, I trusted there would be no sudden road obstacles or loose gravel, trusted in my ability to maneuver the bike at high speeds, and trusted that I would not suffer a catastrophic tire blowout. Sunday, July 21, 1974, required a different trust.

After painstakingly unsewing, patching and resewing two tires we were each left with one good tire and one 'slow-leaker'. Our previous experience in desert biking since descending from Tioga Pass 10 days earlier had taught us a lesson about the scarcity of water and bike shops, as well as the bountiful opportunities for flat tires. Henry Kissinger, Nixon's Secretary of State, said that "the absence of alternatives clears the mind marvelously." It was clear that we had a high likelihood of being stranded in the desert and in need of an emergency hitchhike. So, with loaded bikes at our side, we made a sign for a destination 250 miles across the desert, stuck out our thumbs and re-entered the hitchhiker's world of trust and risk. We would ultimately have to hitch rides on eight occasions for nearly 600 miles. This sounds like a lot – but hey, our legs and wheels got us the remaining 2,968 miles.

In less than 15 minutes a beat-up VW Van pulled over and a very mellow looking, ponytailed, 18-year-old guy named Norman pulled over in a cloud of desert dust.

"Hey dudes! Where ya headed?", said Norman.

Through the rolled down window a cloud of ganja wafted into the air with an aroma reminiscent of my college dorm on any given weekend. This is the part of the memoir where I reveal a deeply secret truth: I have never smoked or eaten marijuana in any form in all of my 70 years on earth. It was illegal in 1974 and I didn't want to risk getting caught in a campus pot bust ruining any chance of getting into med school. After that I just didn't see the need to try it, and it became a personal deprivation of choice. Perhaps a lingering Catholic sacrifice thing that invaded my psyche after inhaling way too much burning incense as an altar boy? Nonetheless, when Norman said that he was headed to Durango as well we jumped into the van faster than Cheech and Chong would have. Unlike Bill Clinton, I never smoked marijuana, but I did inhale the van atmosphere.

To say that hitchhiking was a common mode of transportation for us in high school and college would be an understatement. I hitchhiked to or from school if I missed the city bus, or home from swim team practice, or anywhere really that it would take too long to ride my bike. In the early 1970's hitchhiking was largely practiced by students during daylight hours. In the ultimate display of trust, young people stuck out their thumb and implicitly trusted that a well-meaning, friendly person would pick them up. The motorist possessed a similar measure of trust that the hitchhiker would do them no harm and might even be a bit interesting to chat with.

In 1974 a Welch journalist and English teacher interviewed 700 hitchhikers as they sought a ride, and another 186 hitchhikers that he personally gave a lift to. He found that 33% said their parents approved, 35% said their parents were worried or disapproved, and only 23% said their parents didn't mind or disapprove. I never really had a conversation about hitchhiking with my parents and assumed that they knew how I got around. I'm pretty sure they would have admonished me to NOT hitchhike on the bike trip, even if they never heard of the Santa Rosa California Hitchhiker Murders of 1972-73.

The question of risk and crime in hitchhiking was addressed by the 1974 California Hitchhiking Study – which I never saw until 50 years later. I would have used it to counter any parental concerns had I known about it. This study conducted by the California Highway Patrol (some officers of which we had personally chatted with on days 4 and 5), reviewed serious crimes against or by hitchhikers between May and October 1973. In the Introduction they stated:

> "At first glance, hitchhiking appears to be a desirable mode of transportation. It provides transportation to practically any place in the United States for people who might not otherwise be able to afford to go. In addition, it provides a system of emergency transportation for motorists whose cars become disabled. There is presently a shortage of gasoline which may become increasingly severe. Hitchhiking would be a way to increase the efficiency of automotive transportation. Our society has generally discouraged

> hitchhiking through laws and persuasion. It is felt that a great deal of crime is associated with hitchhiking." [11]

They went on to find 2,028 crimes where hitchhikers were victims, and 800 crimes where hitchhikers were the perpetrators. While females comprised only 9-12% of hitchhikers, they were 7-10 times more likely to be the victims of crime than male hitchhikers. Nearly all the crimes against female hitchhikers were sexual in nature, while robbery was the most common crime against male hitchhikers. I guess our bikes and Burger Chef coupons could have been targets for highway robbery, but I'm sure our often-flattening sew-up tires would have left them cursing and wishing they never robbed us. As far as hitchhikers committing crimes against the driver – they were mostly robbery and theft with only 12% being assault. The study's authors concluded that only 0.63% of the crimes committed in California involved hitchhikers.

We would have knowingly accepted this risk,

had we known the numbers. Like many things, we remained innocently ignorant. We unknowingly embraced the future philosophy of 2024 blogger Max Neumegen. He believes "The hitchhiker is there so you can do your good deed for the day, to share a ride in the same direction." [12] Max even labeled hitchhiking with a bike as the "ultimate way to travel". [12]

We were confident that hitchhiking across the bikeshopless desert was worth the risk. We trusted that our circuitous western route would still ultimately enable us to pedal almost 3,000 miles – just over the distance from San Francisco, California to Ocean City, Maryland of 2939 miles.

So why don't we see much hitchhiking 50 years later? British researchers Graeme Chesters from Edge Hill University College and David Smith, Professor of Social Work at Lancaster University posed this very question in their paper The Neglected Art of Hitchhiking. They felt the decline in hitchhiking was due to the increase in car ownership and societal views of one's car as private mobile space. Drivers who personally hitchhiked and liked to pick up thumbers out of nostalgia steadily declined. There was also the increased fear by hitchhikers and by lift-givers of crime, fueled by movies such as Kalifornia in 1993 where Brad Pitt is a psychopath hitchhiker ironically picked up by a grad student and his girlfriend researching murder sites of serial killings. Or The Hitchhiker in 2007 where four women driving to Las Vegas pick up a seemingly friendly hitchhiker, who isn't. Over the years we students and other 'familiar looking people' stopped hitchhiking, and the roads were left to people with no alternative transportation due to transgressions like repeated DUIs, revoked driver licenses or repossessed cars. Increasingly, folks who hitchhiked became viewed as "marginal, deviant, possibly criminal and certainly risky." What a bummer.

Miraculously, a group called Hitchwiki.org has now popped up on the scene to revitalize hitchhiking. Hitchwiki is a collaborative, edited, online guide to hitchhiking whose website is replete with stories, research, and how-to advice on solo and even 'group hitchhiking'. What would a modern experience of anything be without an online platform to share pictures and details of your personal hitchhiking experiences? So, there is of course Hitchlog. Could the internet revive our 1974 lost art of hitchhiking? I'm not so sure. I definitely don't want my grandkids trying it out just yet. I'd rather they learn how to ride a bike.

Given Norman's appetite enhanced condition, he drove slowly, and we made frequent stops to eat and get gas (even though the tank wasn't near empty). He stopped in Kayenta on the Navajo Reservation and picked up an old girlfriend. With the addition of her frequent bathroom breaks, and a short detour to stand on the Four Corners monument, we didn't arrive in Durango till after sunset. We all ate dinner at an A&W and while Norman and his girlfriend went out to paint the night, Bob and I pitched a tent behind a Holiday Inn dog kennel next to a river.

Woof ! Woof! Not much sleep that night.

Chapter 12

Navajo Regrets and a Colorado Catastrophe

Day 19 July 22

Durango, Colorado to Pagosa Springs, Colorado: 65 miles

I cannot recall spending any time reflecting on how the Painted Desert got its color or the unique landscape of the high desert that I observed as we hitchhiked the 250 miles from Cameron, Arizona to the Four Corners and Mesa Verde. In retrospect, I truly regret the way that I rather mindlessly traversed this part of America gazing out of a hippie van window. I couldn't see all of it as we drove through some during the night. I also never saw the unrecognized racial bias that I possessed. I was not in the mindset of cross-country hiker Andrew Forsthoefel who carried a sign on his backpack reading "Walking to Listen". I was in the mindset of stoically sticking to our map and getting across a hot, sparsely populated section of Route 140 to a town with a bike shop. Necessary – perhaps. Regrets - definite.

The lands of Navajo Nation cover over 27,000 square miles in Arizona, Utah, and New Mexico, an area larger than 10 states including my own West Virginia. My lack of cultural awareness in 1974 was why I knew so little about this huge swath of America that we had to navigate across. It would take another 20 years for me to learn about the Navajo peoples and their land through the novels of Tony Hillerman, and another 40 years for me to understand the Indigenous experience more deeply through my extended family.

What I recalled in my journal was the desert

being “dry, barren, wasteful and god forsaken” and “pretty colorful in its own right too, but I wouldn’t want to be one of the many Indians who live here all year”. I cringe at reading these words now. What I recall “seeing” was expanses of dry appearing earth with clumps of buffalo grass, and paintbrush, with scattered cholla cactus, and juniper and small piñon pines. There were occasional ribbons of distant green cottonwood trees that I assumed lined a river or creek, while wondering how water could exist out there. In the distance were flat topped mesas with walls of salmon and brown and further away the mountain peaks. I recall scattered homesteads with one story wooden shacks and some round structures I would later learn were hogans. Small corrals held sheep or a few horses. Vast stretches of barbed wire fencing lined the roadsides and occasionally divided large spreads of land.

As college student at age 20, I should have known more about the history of Native Americans than from cowboy and Indian movies. More than the "Manifest Destiny" legend of westward expansion by white Americans who had to deal with 'marauding Indians' and 'scalping savages." I was uneducated in the Navajo perspective of an indigenous culture centuries old that underwent Kit Carson's scorched earth and starvation genocide strategy. Scores of Native Americans were brutally forced to relocate. Did the Navajo individuals that we encountered assume that I knew of the 1864 'Long Walk' where over 9,000 men, women and children were forced to walk 300 miles from Arizona to Bosque Redondo near Fort Sumner, New Mexico? Did they assume (correctly) that I was unaware that they became the rare tribe that successfully negotiated a return to their traditional lands between the four sacred mountains? Instead, I found myself disappointingly echoing the opinion of U.S. General Tecumseh Sherman that the Navajo Nation lands were worthless and desolate and "as far from our future possible wants as it is possible to determine." Journalist Ta-Nehisi Coates writes "Race is the child of racism, not the father." This perspective holds that first white men exploited people for their land, labor or access to resources, not according to how they looked or spoke. The ideology of unequal races then followed to justify the exploitation.

What I regrettably did not see were the small canyons, hidden gardens, and arroyos, or the inside of a hogan with its earthen dome, center smoke hole, and eastward facing door so that first sight in the morning is the rising sun. I never got off my bike to see a petroglyph on a smooth deep red canyon wall. I did not "see" how miles of barbed wire fence were the antithesis of Navajo farming and shepherding traditions. Yet, 20 years later I was able to learn some of the much that I missed in Navajo Nation and culture from Tony Hillerman's novels. His vivid descriptions of the Navajo landscape in which his crime stories took place, and his outsider insights into Diné culture and ceremonies were far more revealing than the academic history books of my 1970s eastern US schooling. Thirty years later The Jim Thorpe Story ('the world's greatest athlete and member of the Sac and Fox tribe) introduced me to the shocking practice of 'boarding schools' where children were forcibly removed from their homes and placed in boarding schools far from their families. Stripped of their traditional garments, adornments and long hair they were 'educated' in an attempt to destroy any threads of their tribal culture. This cruelty and abuse were imposed on Navajos beginning in the 1930s and incredibly some Indian boarding schools were still in existence while we were blindly bicycling out West in 1974.

It took my stepdaughter Kristen, a tribally enrolled Apache, to teach me about the importance of knowing your indigenous history and roots. She was adopted by my wife Peg as an infant during her first marriage. During what is both of our second marriages, we shared the tumult of her teenage identity search. Thankfully, we are now witnessing the emergence of her 'Hozho', or living in harmony, with her marriage to her Navajo writer and musician Pete as they carve out their new life in Moab, Utah. I had the honor of using my academic grant writing skills to land her some funding to build resilience and community through her non-profit Native Youth Alliance and Nourishing Traditions programs. I came to understand the effect of past colonialism on Native Americans, and the social ills that followed their separation from the grounding traditions and language of their cultures. Understanding the 'Why' for her projects and helping her help other Native Americans helped salve some of my Navajo regrets I suppose. But the process was not always easy.

I have learned about a controversial term called "white fragility" which explains some of the discomfort and anxiety I have always experienced in conversations about race. It stems from the realization and subtle sense of guilt when being honest about the mantle of entitlement and advantage that I enjoyed in my white rural-suburban culture. Rather shocking to think about, and a term that needles the emotions of defensiveness. Author Robin Diangelo suggests that we need to gradually build our capacity to live with "the discomfort of racial humility'. I have never considered myself to be a racist and although my father occasionally used some the racial vernacular of his times – I was raised to believe that all people are equal and deserving. I now see that racism does indeed exist as a system that arose from one racial group's prejudice backed by legal authority and institutional control.

It was all right there in front of me as I sped through Navajo Nation in a van with the beautiful star filled skies above - but I did not really get the picture. I could be benevolent and feel that "I don't have a racial bone in my body", but there still exist some systematic defaults that perpetuate racism. My culture has racial bones in its body, and I need to realize this. In 1974 I would have declared with my college education that racism was surely a vanishing concept in our country. Anyone could become anything in American, and all that. I regret that 50 years later the ugly divided politics in our great country is vividly exploiting racism.

The first thing we did in Durango was to hit a bakery. We ate at a lunch wagon after devouring the melt in your mouth glazed donuts and wandered around the picturesque mountain town. It was clean, and friendly, with flyers on telephone poles advertising youth activities and green parks that reminded me of back home. Blocks from the bike shop a friendly looking guy our age rolled up to us on his sew-up tire equipped 10-speed and marveled that we were able to ride with loaded panniers on sew-ups.

"How many spares do you carry with you?" asked the long-haired biker sporting a green biker short-billed cap.

"None right now," I replied. "We're headed to the bike shop to get some."

"Right on! I used to work there and can sell you two of the sew-up tires that I have in my pack," he incredibly offered.

So, at fifteen dollars a tire we purchased the new looking tires and smiled at our good fortune. Our smiles turned to embarrassment as we visited the bike shop and saw the same sew-ups for sale at seven dollars apiece. "That little f#!&*!" I thought upon learning that we had been ripped off. But even that would not spoil our celebration of being out of the desert and on to another mail stop in Bayfield, Colorado.

I put the Durango swindle out of my mind and enjoyed the day's 600-foot elevation gain over 65 miles. The mail stop satiated our chocolate chip cookie cravings, and the distant peaks, blue skies and mountain flowers promised a lovely end to our day until it happened again.

Within one mile Bob and I both got flat tires. This time we were then riding on our only tires - with no spares.

"I don't know how much longer we can limp

along with these darn sew up tires," said an exasperated Bob.

"We have to climb another 3,700-feet of elevation to make it over the Continental Divide at Wolf Creek Pass tomorrow, and then make it to Alamosa. We should find a bike shop there," I replied with waning confidence.

I didn't really answer Bob's question. We both knew our tire situation was a catastrophe lurking around the next bend.

Chapter 13

Almost Alamosa

Day 20 July 23

Pagosa Spgs, CO to Alamosa, CO: 83 miles (35 by pickup)

Survivalist Laurence Gonzales says to hold on to your plan with a gentle grip. On Day 20 we were still clutching to our lightweight sew up tire plan with the tightness of my little grandkids clutching my hand on the way to get a promised ice cream cone. After spending $30.00 for a new set of new tubular tires in Durango we only made it another 65 miles before we each got a flat and were down to our last tires – with no spares.

"OK Bob, today our lucks' gotta change. Let's see what it's like once we get over the Continental Divide," I offered.

"Yeah, but this getting old, and starting to really chew up our money", replied Bob with the sober insight of a future CPA.

Our luck did indeed change - it got worse. Bob popped five rear wheel spokes and barely made it up Wolf Creek Pass with his wobbling wheel resembling the guys staggering out of the casino back in Tonopah, Nevada.

"There's no way I can ride down this mountain safely," lamented Bob at the summit.

He stuck out his thumb and quickly caught a ride from a guy heading to Del Norte, CO.

"There's no way I can pass up this long descent after coming uphill all this way. Ok if I ride on and meet you in De Norte?" I admittedly half announced, and half asked.

Soon Bob was carefully removing his front wheel, stuffing his bike and panniers in the back seat and headed down the mountain on four wheels instead of two.

I raced down the eastern side of the mountain - riding alone, but not lonely - in solitude but not isolated. I shifted onto the large chainring and tucked down for the descent. Tears rolled from my eyes in the streaming wind as I let the wheels run when my pedaling could not match my increasing speed. Within 5 miles it rained, snowed, hailed and the sun shone. It was glorious. Then the uneven pavement caused a telltale clunk from my rear tire, and I realized that I had a not-so-slow leak in my new rear sew up tire. The remaining downhill ride was anything but glorious. I had to ride a mile, stop and pump, and repeat – until me and my tire were too pooped to pump any more.

A kind cowboy named Tom saw me sitting on the roadside looking exhausted with my cylindrical silver bike pump and its dangling rubber tube connector in hand. He picked me up a few miles outside of Del Norte and as we rolled into town, we saw Bob sitting on the corner curb at Grand and Oak Street.

"Shall we wave and drive on by him?" said Tom with a bit of a sinister grin.

"No, I think we should pick him up cause I have a long way to ride with him, and he's carrying our dinner," I replied – hoping he was just kidding. So, we pulled over, Bob loaded his bike in the pickup bed, and we continued on to Alamosa.

We almost made it to Alamosa on those fancy lightweight sew-up tires and wheels but after 1,572 miles it was time for a parting of the ways. The Alamosa Fix-It-Shop was ready to close on that Tuesday late afternoon as we pulled up to the storefront. We said our thanks and goodbye to the kind cowboy with the

Denver Bronco orange pick-up truck and went inside the shop as the lights were being turned off. The young couple that ran the shop indulged us enough to hear our predicament, and then our luck changed, again.

"You're in luck. I do have the new rims, spokes, clincher tires and tubes that you need, but there's just one problem. There is no way I can do all that work till later in the week" said Gary the young suntanned proprietor who was living the mountain dream.

"Well, what if we told you that we ran a bike shop back in West Virginia and could do all the labor ourselves if you could just let us use your shop," I replied with fingers crossed.

Gary looked over his John Lenon spectacles and replied, "OK, cool, but you would have to do it tonight when I'm closed, 'cause like I said, I have so much work I have to do this week".

After some bartering on price, we found ourselves grimy and sweaty, with hands happily covered in grease as we dismantled our wheels spoke by spoke under the workbench lights of the Alamosa Fix-It-Shop. Surrounded by tools, bicycles and walls adorned with everything from sizing charts to poems and aphorisms – we were like elves in Santa's workshop. Fortuitously, we encountered no frozen nipples, not the frostbite injury dreaded by winter distance runners, the rusted tight threaded nipples that hold the spoke in the wheel rim. With Gary's bicycle mechanic manual in hand, we tackled the symmetrical front wheels first, as opposed to the shorter spokes needed for one side of the rear wheels to accommodate the space taken up by the freewheel cluster. We faithfully laced the spokes layer by layer until we had created the strong cross 3 pattern. Wheel by wheel we worked late into the night.

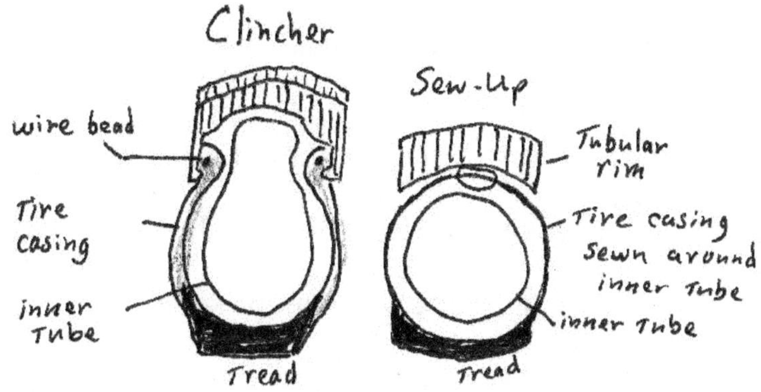

Anatomy of Clincher vs Sew-Up Rims and Tires

"How would you guys like a little help?" said Gary who appeared back at the shop at 12:30 am.

"Are you kidding? Sure!" Bob and I replied in unison with our hoarse fatigued voices.

Gary placed each wheel on the trueing stand and methodically tweaked each spoke nipple until all four wheels spun without bump or wobble. The final step of installing the new tubes and tires was joyous.

"You do know that you never should have used those sew up tires?" said Gary with a smirk.

"Well, let's just say that our experiment failed, and you rescued us," I replied.

The abandonment of our sew-up tires was a relief and an embarrassment. Kind of like Meriwether Lewis of Lewis and Clark fame who spent several months in Harpers Ferry (now West Virginia) collaborating with the armory workers to construct a collapsable iron framed boat. Meriwether had designed it along with Thomas Jefferson and was quite proud of this innovation. The Armory also produced the Harpers Ferry Model 1803 rifle, the first regulation US Army rifle, and Lewis bought 15 of these prototypes for the Expedition.

Merriwether and the skilled iron craftsmen built a lightweight but large canoe frame that would be covered with animal hides and sealed with tar pitch when needed. The prototype frame weighed only 44 pounds and supported a load of 1,770 lbs. His boat was called "Experiment", and sadly, it failed. When he tried to assemble it at the Great Falls of the Missouri River it leaked like a sieve as he had no tar pitch to properly seal the hide seams. "Experiment" was abandoned on the banks of the river, and the iron frame was never recovered.

Bob and I abandoned our sew-up tires lightweight rims in Alamosa, Colorado, also never to be recovered. Twenty years after our adventure of 1974, I embarked on my own Harpers Ferry 'Experiment'. Together with my family practice partners Dr Rosemarie Cannarella, MD and Linda Shields, MD, we joined forces with the West Virginia University School of Medicine and designed a family medicine specialty training program. This three-year residency program enrolled small groups of doctors and provided their medical training in the rural panhandle of West Virginia. The idea was that doctors who trained in small towns and communities would be more apt to locate their future practices in rural underserved areas. Our two regional hospitals and many physicians and their clinic staffs in Berkeley and Jefferson counties met the challenge and provided a fantastic medical education experience for our bold pioneer residents. I am happy to report that our Harpers Ferry 'Experiment' was a success and grew into what is now the Eastern Division of the WVU School of Medicine where I was blessed to practice, teach, and administrate from 1994 to 2017.

Our new clinchers seemed armor thick compared to our failed experiment lightweight sew up tires. My sleep deprived brain assured me that we would never get another flat for the next 2,000 miles. We spent the remaining night sleeping on the floor of the apartment above the bike shop. We were extended this gift by Juan, a grad student with a great taste in music. I quickly fell asleep and had a surreal dream of biking up a mountain with my new clincher tires and being passed by a professional cyclist with sew-up tires. The cyclist sarcastically said as he passed me by "Bella pneumatici" ("Nice wheels!"). "Il tuo" ("Up yours") I replied in perfect Italian. He was followed by a red Fiat carrying 4 new wheels, a replacement bike, and their Italian mechanic, Swedish masseuse, Belgian manager, and French nutritionist all hanging out the widows shouting in their native tongues.

After 5 hours of sleep, I woke up thankful that we almost made it to Alamosa with blowout prone skinny sew-up tires and no sarcastic European support crew. Juan cooked us an omelet breakfast and sent us on our way with a batch of cookies.

I will never forget the kindness we experienced in Alamosa, CO, nor the feeling that we were almost at the half-way point on our time schedule and still not even halfway across Colorado.

Chapter 14

Mascots and Sunsets

Day 21 July 24

Alamosa, Colorado to Walsenburg, Colorado: 73 miles

Day 22 July 25

Walsenburg, CO to Las Animas, Colorado: 83 miles

Day 23 July 26

Las Animas, Colorado to Holly, Colorado 75 miles

Day 24 July 27

Holly, Colorado to Kalvesta, Kansas: 95 miles

With new clincher tires and wheels, we felt invincible. Our renewed confidence powered us up our final Rocky Mountain summit at the 9,459 feet elevation

North La Venta Pass. The miles started to fly by once we dropped into the plains of eastern Colorado. We reached our mail stop, 142 miles later, at Hasty, Colorado, and loaded up on cookies sent from home. The next stop was Lamar, Colorado – a small town where my future eldest son, Ryan, would serve as their hospitals' locum tenens (part-time fill in) anesthesia provider. Admittedly, in 1974 I was unphased by their high school 'Lamar Savages' athletic schedule posted in town. However, forty-five years later when Ryan visited the local bakery, he was shocked to see cakes frosted with the 'Lamar Savages' moniker. Today it seems obvious that the term 'savages' was not coined in homage to the American Indian. The school board clung to their racially demeaning mascot until Colorado passed a law prohibiting the use of American Indian mascots by public schools and public institutions of higher education. The act imposed a fine of $25,000 per month for each month that a public school continued to use an American Indian mascot. This gave birth to the current 'Lamar Thunder' and its charging buffalo mascot. It seems the school board calculated that they could no longer afford their bigotry, however, their history remains. The high school still resides on the corner of Savage Avenue and Thunder Drive. Apparently, you can't legislate attitude or street names.

On Day 23 we pedaled on to Holly, Colorado, 4 miles from the Kansas State Line - and it was sweet. Naturally, because we were in the home of the Holly Sugar Company which began harvesting sugar beets in 1905 and by 1974 had multiple sugar refining operations across several western states. In 1988 Imperial Sugar (which refined sugar cane in Texas) merged with Holly Sugar, but by 2024 there is no longer a sugar beet industry in Holly or eastern Colorado. 50 years later the population is barely above 800 residents.

Agriculture has always been risky in southeastern Colorado, mostly due to inconsistent water for irrigation. The Colorado River water that has caused such controversy in its allocation to Arizona, Nevada, and California – has headwaters from the Roaring Fork and Frying Pan rivers on what is called "the western slope" of Colorado. Areas east of the continental divide are called "the eastern slope", and in eastern Colorado and western Kansas they get little water from the snowpack on their side of the mountain.

In 1974 as we biked through this drought-stricken area, work was progressing on a series of dams, canals and Continental Divide tunnels that in 2024 divert water from the western slope of the Rockies over to the eastern slope. This water never reaches its nature intended south westward flowing Colorado River. The Fryingpan-Arkansas Project commissioned in 1962 by President Kennedy is still incomplete and unable to deliver adequate water to the western Arkansas River Valley (The river runs through Colorado, Kansas, Oklahoma, and finally Arkansas where it meets the Mississippi). In 2024 high levels of minerals leaching from the areas poorly diluted aquafers leak selenium, radium and uranium into the groundwater of many southeastern Colorado communities who depend on well water.

The complexity and controversy lie in the nature blessed water produced by the mountainous western slopes with little flat farmland. Conversely, the eastern slopes and Colorado plains have farmable land and room to grow but very little water. Western slope extremists feel that if God had wanted crops grown in eastern Colorado, he would have provided the water to do it. Eastern slope and Colorado plains extremists feel that Colorado water is being sent to other states to their detriment. I feel fortunate (but not too guilty) to be able to enjoy fishing in the rushing waters of the Roaring Fork River near Glenwood Springs, Colorado. It is where the one-time Lamar nurse anesthesiologist son Ryan, his family, and my wife Peg and I, now call home.

As the Rockies receded from our rear view, the wide-open plains of Kansas stretched far into the eastern horizon. Furrows of farmland, crop tops doing 'the wave' in the wind, and a new air of solitude greeted us. Bad news for farmers - no rain there since June 8. Bad news for us - coarse asphalt with stretches of expansion cracks every 20 feet. Each bump wounded my healing rump. Nonetheless, we amassed multiple sequential days over 75 miles. We often pedaled late into the evening and watched gold and red sunsets before camping in soft grass off in a quiet field.

It started to feel like we would actually make it to the Atlantic Ocean by mid-August.

Chapter 15

A Madonna Encounter and a Melanoplus Attack

Day 25 July 28

Kalvesta, Kansas to Great Bend, KS: 104 miles (45 by car)

Day 26 July 29

Great Bend, Kansas to Marion, Kansas: 101 miles

We hit our record 22 miles in one hour in Kansas. Of course, that's when a massive thunderstorm raced in from the east, forcing us to take shelter in a culvert under the road. We emerged from the culvert like wet rats and were greeted by 20 mph headwinds. Forty-one-year-old Mikey had just motorcycled over our route through Nevada and Arizona, and upon seeing us fellow road warriors he was compelled to pull over. He sported a biker's sunburnt face and forearms, as well as a beer drinker's belly earned in off-road activities.

"Hey guys! How would you like to get outa this wind? I can give you a lift into the next town," he yelled over the raging gusts.

His small trailer was empty having sold his motorcycle, so, we loaded up our bikes and hopped into his car. We laughed and exchanged stories about our summer road travels.

"So, you went from Yosemite to Las Vegas. So did we. Wasn't Yosemite amazing?" I asked.

Mikey replied "I had great weather and could have ridden around those turns and cliffs all day. I bet it was tougher for you guys on bikes humping up those mountains."

"Sure was, especially in the pouring rain," said Bob. "But it was worth it."

"How about riding over the Hoover Dam? So cool, and an older couple even made us this big picnic lunch at the top of that hill on the Arizona side," I chimed in.

"Yeah, the Hoover Dam was awesome," said Mikey. "I crossed it during the night and wanted to pee over the edge of the dam, but those signs warned you to keep off the wall, and I didn't want to get arrested!"

"I wonder how many seconds it would have taken for your pee to hit the bottom?" queried Bob.

We howled at the thought of big Mikey standing on the Hoover Dam wall peeing over the side while cop cars sped toward him, sirens blaring. Another great encounter ended as he dropped us off at a Great Bend, Kansas roadside picnic area. We said our goodbyes and he pulled off into the sunset.

The storm and trailing winds had abated, and the sun was approaching the horizon in another gold and orange spectacle. We pitched our tent near a raucous Hispanic family picnic. Before the last stake was pounded into the hard dirt, we heard a lovely sound.

"Hey amigos! Want a beer?" beckoned Pancho, the family patriarch.

He was dressed in pointy-toed cowboy boots, and blue jeans held up by a big shiny belt buckle with a bucking bronco on it. His belly overlapped his belt a bit behind the tucked, crisp, white button-down western shirt. A smile beamed out from under his mustache. He held up two open bottles of Coors and waved us over to his picnic tables. That Sunday evening, we were treated to the best in Mexican picnic cuisine and unlimited beer that this boisterous restaurant owner could offer. His family treated us like long lost sons who hadn't eaten in months. Stories of our biking escapades, his restaurant business, the drought, and funny family stories lasted till nearly midnight.

This was the first time I experienced the warmth and joy of a large family since the last family dinner I had with my six siblings, aunt, uncle, and parents before we left for our trip. It felt good. I wondered how that California kid could have been so disparaging about Mexicans.

"So, Pancho, when did you come to Kansas?" I asked.

"We have been here over ten years, and me and my family have built the restaurant from the ground up, "he proudly replied.

"To tell you the truth, I don't think there are any Mexicans where we come from in West Virginia. We just heard about Mexican apricot workers when we were in California, but never met anyone from Mexico till you."

Without the Coors I don't think I would have had

the balls to say something like that. Pancho and his wife both cracked an uncomfortable smile. His older children who were paying attention just looked at us. Bob glanced at me with a 'what did you just say?' look in his eyes. Did I just offend the entire family who had been so nice to us? Did I sound like I thought Mexicans only worked in the fields? Why did I ever bring any of this up?

Pancho finally broke the painful seconds of silence.

"Yeah, that's the kind of work that brings many from my country to America, but not me. I am a businessman, a restaurant owner, and Mexico has many people like me as well. So, what do you think about that?" he said with his big smile peeking out from under his bushy mustache once again.

"I think you have an awesome family, and with food like this, your restaurant must be a big success," I replied.

Bob raised his beer and rescued the evening with a "Cheers!".

"!Salud!" rang out from the drinking adults and the conversation returned to more mundane topics like 'where are you headed tomorrow' and ' my cousin lives there, maybe you will see him'. The party broke up with Pancho announcement.

"Everyone, it's time to go home – there is work to do in the morning, and our Gringo bicycle friends need some sleep."

We heartily shook hands with our host and sincerely thanked Pancho and his family for inviting us to join them. Minus my stupid comments, it was a great end to a weird day. I learned that those who are outsiders or minorities are more comfortable than me in talking about the differences and stereotypes that they live with every day.

I'm not sure if we would have spontaneously walked over to Pancho's picnic and struck up a conversation. It was he who reached out and invited us to join his family outing – a genuinely gracious man.

The sun rose hot in the morning sky and our Day 26 ride across Kansas continued. In Council Grove, Kansas a large roadside sculpture caught my eye, and we screeched to a halt. It was a Madonna of the Trail statue! The same towering pioneer woman I passed hundreds of times on Route 40 National Road near a park entrance in my hometown of Wheeling, West Virginia. She is wearing a bonnet and intrepidly cradling a baby in her left arm, and a rifle in her right hand, as a small child clings to her long dress. In the past I played terrible golf on the public course behind her, watched my cousin from Seattle wrap a driver around a tree in frustration, and relieved myself in the long-needled pines that gracefully surround the monument site.

Madonna of the Trail, Council Grove, Kansas

On a more historically significant note, twelve identical Madonnas of the Trail were commissioned by the National Society, Daughters of the American Revolution in 1911. Harry S. Truman (a Missouri judge at the time) led the committee which selected locations for the statues along the National Road (Rt 40) and Santa Fe Trail (Rt 66). These 5-ton statues are located in

Maryland, Pennsylvania, West Virginia, Ohio, Indiana, Illinois, Missouri, Kansas, Colorado (apparently, we missed the one in Lamar), New Mexico, Arizona and California. I can only imagine the politicking that went on among those DAR ladies to get a Madonna erected in their towns.

A statue design by August Leimbach (which he created with 3-days' notice) was selected. This 1910 German immigrant was an architect and master sculpturer He carved the original Madonna from clay and casted the monuments from algonite, a mixture of marble, granite, stone, cement, and lead ore. He was paid $1,000 per statute and all twelve were completed and dedicated between 1928 and 1929. Leimbach went on to teach at Washington University, and create architectural sculptures on many St Louis buildings, as well as wood carvings and paintings for churches and other institutions. In a sad story of politics, war, and immigration – this gifted contributor to American culture had not become a US citizen, so he was faced with imprisonment in a detention camp or returning to Germany as World War II began. He left his adult children behind in St Louis and returned to Germany with his wife. At the conclusion of the war his country was split into East and West Germany and the Russians jailed him for being an enemy of the state. He was eventually freed by the jail's townspeople and lived in Germany until his death in 1963 – he was 83 years old. During World War I, German immigrants were called Huns and accused of not assimilating into America. During World War II American's feared Leimbach that German immigrants were spies, or possibly loyal to Hitler. Hitler allegedly proclaimed he would gladly send the US uneducated, criminal German Jews in a luxury liner, if needed. In 2024 some politicians claim, without evidence, that Central American governments are sending us their criminals. I wonder if any modern August Leimbachs are among our current immigrants. The Madonna of the Trail monuments inscription states – she is

"… the pioneer mother of America through whose courage and sacrifice the desert has blossomed. The camp became a home, the blazed trail the thoroughfare…. Into the primitive west, face up swung toward the sun, bravely she came, her children beside her, here she made a home, beautiful pioneer mother."

As we spun away from her down the Santa Fe Trail, I ruminated on the conditions that she must have endured – rutted roads, wind, rain, drought, and locusts. I thought my mother would certainly have been a Madonna of the Trail had she and my father ventured west with their seven children in the 1800s.

Town streets led again to the open road flanked by juvenile corn stalks with afternoon grasshoppers occasionally flittering out from the fields. Serenely lost in thought, I pedaled along.

Suddenly, "What the f#?* !"

I didn't know what hit me at first. Maybe a rock?

I wiped my searing, soaked cheek, expecting to see bright red arterial blood. Instead, there was the unmistakable brown slime of grasshopper 'tobacco spit'. I saw this many times as a kid on Locust Avenue as we collected grasshoppers in jars for mass execution. (yes, little boys can be stupidly cruel). Had I entered Rod Serling's Twilight Zone, and this was the start of one of those old TV westerns where settlers were besieged by sky blackening grasshopper swarms?

Well, it turns out that the great Grasshopper Plague of July 1874 descended upon Kansas on the very ground that I was traversing. Millions of so called "Rocky Mountain Locusts" (aka *Melanoplus spretus*) reportedly chewed through their crops, fabrics, and even the wool off of living sheep. Smaller swarms appeared over the years but as mysteriously as they came – they disappeared. The last reported live Rocky Mountain locust was seen in 1902, and they were officially declared extinct in 2014. Farming, irrigation, trampling by cattle, and floods are thought to have destroyed their usual egg laying grounds and collectively caused the demise of this species.

Undoubtedly that lone genetically modern 1974 grasshopper was destined to recreate the attack his ancient relatives waged 100 years earlier by whacking me in the face and spewing his 'tobacco spit'. Like Madonna of the Trail, I survived.

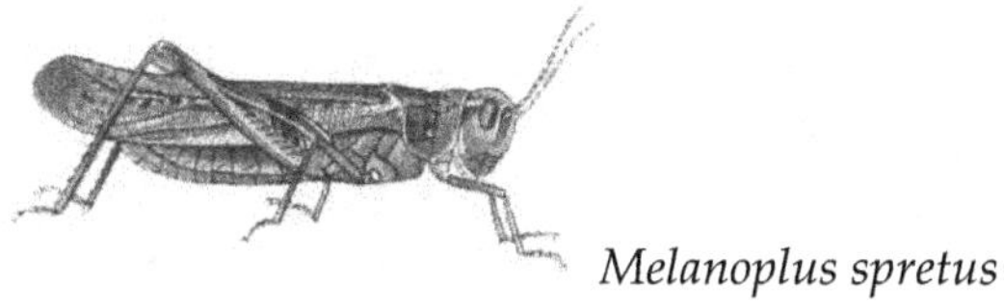

Melanoplus spretus

While she trudged westward, Bob and I biked eastward. After a 101-mile day, we camped at Marion Lake outside of Marion, Kansas. We arrived after the check-in office had closed. We woke up early before the office re-opened and avoided paying the camp site fee.

This set Karma into motion.

Chapter 16

Garbage, Silos and Seeking Salvation in Sedalia

Day 27 July 30

Marion, Kansas to Topeka, Kansas:105 miles (30 by pickup)

Day 28 July 31

Topeka, Kansas to Martin City, Missouri: 76 miles

Day 29 August 1

Martin City, Missouri to Sedalia, Missouri: 80 miles

We had another goody-laden mail stop at the Delavan, Kansas post office. After 106 years of service to General Delivery itinerants like us and the good citizens of Morris County, the US Postal Service permanently closed it in 1992. Seventy-five miles later Karma dropped a similar axe on a piece of Bob's bike. There was a loud 'snap', followed by an 'oh no', as Bob came to an abrupt stop.

Karma: his Grand Turismo Campagnolo rear derailleur had broken in two at the jockey wheel arm.

What a way to end Day 27. With only 30 more miles to Topeka, we hitched a ride from some commuting carpenters who dropped us off at the Washburn University campus. We split up to find a friendly fraternity or sorority house. I found Bob an hour and a half later at the Kappa Sigma fraternity house where he had gotten us invited to their spaghetti dinner and secured two sofa beds for the night. Sadly, there were no coed slumber parties to crash.

The next morning Bob bought a new Suntour GT rear derailleur ($9.00) and we were on our way. On Days 28 and 29 we cruised across Kansas and entered

Missouri. Bob and I had a bet going that whoever got the first flat tire on our new clinchers would have to buy the other a beer. Within a few hours Bob got to buy me a nice cold can of beer with beads of perspiration dripping down the sides. It was especially refreshing as the temp hit 105 degrees on July 31 – the hottest day of our journey. It paired well with the 19¢ McDonalds hamburger special across the street. Thanks Bob!

The Midwest topography became very familiar: After a long stretch of lonesome highway first came the farms with cute homes, surrounded by a few shade trees down a long brown road off the highway; then came silos and the town grain towers; then the roadside evidence of human debris; then the bars, gas stations, and light industry; then the schools and residential neighborhoods; then Main Street with its cloak of hopeful renewal, quaint survival or boarded up despair; and then pretty much the reverse pattern upon exiting the town. Of course, the people we would meet were the star attractions, but the litter and the silos were always intriguing to me.

The Keep America Beautiful campaign started the month before I was born, and their 1971 Earth Day theme ‘People Start Pollution. People Can Stop It’ featured the ‘Crying Indian’ ad - where an Italian American actor portrayed a Native American shedding a single tear looking at our litter and pollution. There was still a notable amount of litter along some roadsides in 1974, particularly on the outskirts of towns. I never figured out if people wanted to unload their car trash before entering the town to arrive with a clean vehicle, or if they just chucked shit out the window for a nasty goodbye gesture as they exited.

I worked on a downtown Wheeling garbage truck for the 6 weeks between the spring semester end and our bike trip departure, and therefore could claim to be a bit of a garbage aficionado. I vividly remember the look on my parents’ faces as they pulled their car to a stoplight just as I emerged from one of those below the sidewalk basements of the corner department store. Pop says he turned to my mom and said,

"We'll Jane, there's our oldest son! Makes you proud to see a possible future doctor hauling trash at 7:30 AM."

They were celebrating their wedding anniversary by returning to the same early morning mass at the Cathedral where they were married. I never got a reasonable answer as to why they got married at 7:30 AM, but I am eternally grateful for the way they taught us the value of honest work.

Downtown Wheeling garbage notwithstanding, you could get a clue about the nature of an upcoming Midwest town from their roadside trash. Absence of beer cans – a dry town. McDonalds or Burger Chef wrappers – town probably has at least 5,000 people. Empty French-fry boxes and milkshake cups – high school on this side of town. Empty liquor and beer bottles with crumpled cigarette packs and old butts –

gonna be some poverty and boarded up storefronts. Half a century later there is far less littering, but what roadside debris one finds still tells anthropological tales. While on a 2023 Ride-the-Rockies tour biking up a mountain pass leading to a Colorado cassino town, I passed some scattered spent ammunition cartridges and empty mini-booze bottles. Go figure.

Abandoned Kansas homestead

Far less numerous than discarded food wrappers,

but more interesting, were the silos that dotted the Kansas landscape. I appreciated the nostalgia of the occasional abandoned and lifeless farm with saplings growing out of the glassless house windows and collapsed roof. Nearby stood a brownish red ceramic block silo. I imagined the hard work and sacrifices of those farming families whose dashed dreams must have been so painful to walk away from. The resourcefulness of using the rest of a grain plant to create a storable food source for wintering cattle was certainly lost on me as I consumed my fair share of hamburgers.

I thought silos looked cool and just stored stuff grown on the farm. In fact, silos are used to create silage (try and say that word three times fast), which is fermented green plants. The idea is to pack organic material (like cut up whole corn stalks or alfalfa) into these silos and create an oxygen free environment so that the fermentation process can acidify and preserve the feed. A Carnegie Melon educated farmer, Ron, taught me this many years later back in the eastern panhandle of West Virginia.

"Think of it as sauerkraut for cows - this way the feed won't rot, mold or spoil. "

He showed me silage that he fed his dairy cows, and I can assure you that it did not resemble any sauerkraut that I ever saw on my New Year's Day pork and mashed potato plate.

Of course I didn't know this in 1974, but I did notice that there were way more concrete silos held together with steel bands. Turns out these were far less expensive to build and more airtight than the ceramic block. Yet driving across the Midwest in 2024 I saw very few silos, and many curious rows of huge plastic bags or rolls of hay covered tightly in plastic. This new method is like making many small batches of silage and avoiding the expense and danger of those tall silos.

Farming is a dangerous business. 'Silo fillers lung' is caused by farmers entering the top of a silo and getting severe often fatal lung damage from exposure to the nitrous dioxide produced in the fermentation process. Then there's the possibility of being killed in an explosion. Those grain towers and grain elevators that still stand as town sentinels visible for miles should come with their own 'Can Be Hazardous to Human Health' labels. Grain elevators and their tall storage towers take grain like wheat or oats at the proper moisture content and elevate it up to the top of the structure's headhouse where it is directed to storage towers. There the grain is kept aerated. Farmers can get paid on the spot for their grain or store it for a while waiting for the best price. Unfortunately, the process of conveying the grain up a 70 to 120-foot elevator shaft creates a lot of dust. Combined with ample oxygen and a spark, massive explosions have occurred. In 1974 there were over 20 explosions a year, but improvements in the elevators, ventilation and spark source control have reduced these fatal events dramatically by 2024.

As Kansas turned into Missouri, we hit

unexpected hills and some nasty storms. After a sleepless rainy night in Martin City, Missouri we rolled into Sedalia, Missouri 80 miles later. We were hungry, exhausted and dreading the prospect of spending another all-night rain in a leaky tent. Incredibly, Bob came up with the idea of walking out of the rain into the Sedalia Police Department, and straight up asking if we could spend the night in their jail.

"I'm so tired. I'm gonna do it" Bob declared.

Brilliant! I thought. Something straight out of Andy Griffith of Mayberry. Maybe their Barney Fife would be from Morgantown, WV like Don Knotts. I was delirious with anticipation as Bob sauntered down the hall. He was actually going to ask if we could stay in a jail cell! He went straight up to the station clerk counter where he boldly asked,

"Excuse me sir, but could you give us some information about where we could camp around here?"

"What the f#!&*!" I silently shouted.

"My god. You boys shouldn't be camping on a night like this. Where are you from?" said the wide-eyed clerk.

"We're from West Virginia but now we're attempting to ride bicycles from San Francisco to Ocean City, Maryland", replied Bob.

"Wow that's some trip boys. Well, I tell you what I can do. Here are some 'OK Slips' that will get you into the Salvation Army Transient Center just down the street. It's not luxury accommodations but it's clean and dry and you can sleep there for free."

Bob and I quickly looked at each other and said "Sure! Thank you!" and headed to the nearby building where we waited in line in the entry room with its speckled tiled flooring. The institutional light green cinderblock walls were brightly illuminated by humming overhead fluorescent lighting - a necessity for the elderly woman at the desk to properly examine the people seeking shelter that night. We waited in line as she loudly conversed with two obviously intoxicated men.

"Don't you see ma'am? My friend and I can't stay here tonight. We just need some money to buy a couple of motel rooms," the taller gentleman slurred while leaning on his shorter companion.

"Now why would I give you money to buy a couple of motel rooms"!

"Because we are caring for like eight kids and we can't all fit here," he replied with wafting alcohol breath.

"Well, I think you guys are looking for drinking money, but why don't you just bring in those eight children and we can talk about this some more".

With that, we were advanced to the head of the line and after showing her our 'OK Slips' from the police department we were escorted to a room with three empty bunk beds. We locked up our bikes, secured our gear, got a hot shower, free pudding and cookie snack and crashed.

We awoke the next morning with roommates that must have quietly come in during the night, or we just didn't hear them in our fatigue comas. One looked like a scraggly 40 something guy who had a rough night, and the other a guy our age with a crew cut and neck tattoos. We didn't stick around to chit chat and headed across the street to the Coffee Pot restaurant where we got a $1.25 breakfast - courtesy of the Sedalia Salvation Army.

In 1974 the Salvation Army was, and still is, the largest non-governmental social service organization in America. It just so happens that Sedalia, Missouri has quite a history with the Salvation Army. Rewind the clock back to 1886 and Sedalia was a wide-open, booming, cattle and railroad town, dubbed by some as the 'Sodom and Gomorrah of the nineteenth century'. The actual founder of the Salvation Army himself – Mr.

William Booth – traveled all the way from London, England to establish the Salvation Army post in Sedalia. He was attracted to help their target rich wickedness problem but tragically was assaulted in Sedalia. Later back in London, Booth allegedly died from his wounds. This made him the Salvation Army's first martyr.

While the town has settled down a lot since the 1800's we found their spirit of "saving the poor, destitute and hungry" remained alive and well, and much appreciated by two cross country bicyclists from West Virginia.

I have never looked at the Salvation Army holiday bell ringers and their little red kettles the same.

Chapter 17

Goose Liver, Cemetery Dreams and Big Dreams

Day 30 August 2

Sedalia, Missouri to New Haven, Missouri: 125 miles

Day 31 August 3

New Haven, Missouri to Fairmont City, Illinois: 85 miles

Day 32 August 4

Fairmont City, Illinois to Bluff City, Illinois: 65 miles

Day 33 August 5

Bluff City, Illinois to Terre Haute, Indiana 101 miles

Day 30 was a 125-mile day with a high of 95 degrees. We traversed part of the Lewis and Clark Trail and smelled quite ripe when we pulled into Manoke, Missouri, population 390. Bob's 'Beer in every state' mantra worked well for him as he guzzled two draft beers in the air-conditioned town bar while I waited outside – denied service as I was only 20 years old. My journal entry recalls a Mini-Market score of a "cold can of Bud" followed by "a goose liver and cheese sandwich". For some reason Braunschweiger was called 'goose liver' by working class ethnic Germans in Wheeling, WV and Manoke, MO. This parboiled soft sausage was not actual foie gras. This mixture of pork or beef liver, pork and bacon trimmings, and spices including garlic had one of those simultaneously tasty and repulsive flavors. My father would occasionally buy a few slices from the bald butcher with hairy arms across the street when we lived on Edgington Lane. He savored it on bread with mustard and cheese. We kids were told to not eat it because it was a special treat for Pop. Of course I had to sneak some. After a small portion my taste buds would tell my brain to stop. One bite over this limit would result in gastrointestinal side effects, but I was really hungry after biking 111 miles.

Fifteen minutes later Bob emerged from the bar. I farted memorably and hopped back on the bike for Fairmont City, Illinois. Manoke's population is now down to 188 souls.

Our mail stop was a little more complicated in Robertsville, Missouri, where we again arrived on a weekend to find the post office door locked. The small white clapboard office looked like a one-story addition to a larger two-story home, so we knocked on the house door and were greeted by a grandmotherly woman wearing a sweater on the 100-degree afternoon. She spoke to us through a partially opened door, but as we shared our predicament, she opened the door wide and invited us in. "Once she leaves for the day, she can be hard to reach, but we'll make a few calls to see if we can find somebody to get you boys your mail," she sweetly offered. After calling four people she eventually located the cousin of the sister of the postal clerk who promptly arrived and gave us our letters and care packages. It didn't seem like the official USPS security protocol was being followed – but that was the least of our concerns.

Bob at Robertsville, Missouri Post Office

Missouri had a lot of Burger Kings, and we cashed in the free meal coupons as often as we could, but late-night dining would occasionally lead to bedtime queasiness. Despite feeling like crap, we pushed onward on Day 31 and pedaled through Saint Louis and crossed the Mississippi. We didn't stop to ride up the Gateway Arch because we were rather rudely greeted by the rush hour motorists, and we were tired and hot in the 100-degree heat and nearly matching humidity. Granted we were probably slowing up traffic on the back streets that we rode, and Bob did spill out into the road a bit when he wiped out on some berm cinders. Nonetheless, the Missouri drivers were particularly grumpy and horn happy that dog day of summer.

"Get off the road!" emerged from a passing carload of teens. "Here, eat this!" followed their exhortation as a half-eaten sandwich was launched from their car towards us.

Fortunately, the guy was no Bob Gibson (St. Louis Cardinals Hall of Fame ace pitcher). He missed - and the wet ham, cheese, mustard and tomato splatted and sizzled on the scorching pavement. All in all, we were lucky that this was the only time we encountered hostility that summer.

Good sleep, enabling all 4 stages, including dream filled REM sleep, was hard to come by at times. Rainy nights in a tent, camp sites near softball fields with tournaments lasting till 11:00 PM and intestinal rumblings didn't make it easy. On Day 32, at a $3.00 beef smorgasbord complete with a hot fudge sundae, I found a newspaper that carried a story about a 20-year-old girl who had cycled cross country safely and unmolested by camping in graveyards. Great idea! Our map showed that Bluff City, Illinois had a roadside cemetery just outside of town.

Through a break in the barbed wire fence the cemetery shared with the adjacent corn field, we quietly entered at dusk, leaned our bikes against a tree out of sight from the road, and pitched our tent. We strangely didn't speak much that night, kind of like we were in church I suppose. I slept like a stone – appropriate for the granite memorials around us – and awoke refreshed and absent the typical morning myalgias.13 We silently packed up our gear and shoved off just before dawn –

and never spent another night in a graveyard. It wasn't because it was spooky or haunting – it just didn't feel right.

Cemeteries like we see now have only been around for 300 years. Earlier civilizations put bodies in caves, or atop a mountain, or cremated them or shoved them off a boat at sea and nature took care of the remains. When medieval churches started burying their deceased in nearby fields there were few markers, and the open grassy areas were used for cattle grazing, fairs, and markets. The scourge of plagues producing multiple diseased bodies caused a lasting cultural change in burial practices. Fenced cemeteries located outside of towns were felt to be safer, and the common use of headstones emerged. Legends of grave robbers, hauntings and zombies soon followed and added to the pervasive sense that one should be respectful and a bit weary when visiting a deceased relative's gravesite. I, however, always found cemeteries to be cool places. It was a special treat to be selected to be an altar boy for a funeral. Not only did you get out of class, but the deceased's family often tipped the altar boys. My father even taught me to drive in a cemetery because he figured I couldn't hurt anyone there.

I think our intuition was right to never camp in cemeteries again. In 2024 the City of Portland, Oregon is infamous for homeless tent encampments. At times they seem to be on every open piece of roadside grass in certain areas between the waxing and waning politics of tolerance and prohibition. I felt guilty as I read the KGW8 news piece on Sleeping by the Dead and learned how relatives felt disrespected and fearful when visiting loved ones' gravesites with tents and open sleeping in the Multnomah Park Cemetery. I now know how I would feel if someone was tent camping near my mother and father's gravesites in Wheeling, WV. I likely wouldn't care where they were bicycling to or what their housing situation was. Now big cities are running out of cemetery lots, so cremation and "green burials" are on the rise. We may be returning to those Medieval burial fields with trees and gardens fertilized with the compost of our loved ones.

Unbelievably, to me, as I write this book my name and birthdate are being engraved on a 'His and Hers' combined gravestone at my wife's insistence. Ever since Peggy lost her twin sister in a horrific car accident at the age of 35, she has been moderately obsessed with assuring that her remains end up in the mausoleum next to her twin in Johnstown, Pennsylvania. You can only imagine the conversations about "Shouldn't we be buried together" or "I don't know anybody in Johnstown" or "What if we get cremated". Let's just say that as of 2024 our ashes will reside in both Colorado under the headstone currently being carved, as well as in the Pennsylvania mausoleum. Currently the Catholic church frowns on scattering or splitting one's ashes – but it is apparently forgiven for soldiers blasted apart in war and astronauts disintegrated in reentry accidents – so why not us. We'll be dead and out of the reach of disapproving priests and nuns by that time.

I'm glad I didn't have any cemetery dreams about my 2024 headstone back in August 1974. We had 85 more miles of pedaling to leave Illinois behind and enter Indiana.

I heard on the radio one New Years Eve that our lives would be most affected by the books we would read and the people we would meet in the coming year. Maybe it was an omen on Day 33 that we would meet Billy in Casey, Illinois (the name most people think I am saying when I introduce myself as KC). To say that he was the kind of person that you would hope didn't make eye contact with you if you met him on a street corner in 2024 is an understatement. At first, I didn't see him by a shade tree at the rest stop where we had pulled in for a short break – but Billy sure saw us. He maneuvered his rig right over to us for a chat. He was pedaling a 40-pound Varsity Schwin loaded down with bungy cord attached sacks and bags which he later informed us weighed 70 lbs.

"Hey fellas! I'm Billy. You headed east like me?" he shouted with a friendly but toothless smile.

"Yeah, we sure are. I'm KC and this is Bob," I replied, realizing that on a bike even the most unlikely fellow bikers were brothers.

Minutes later my mind was speeding ahead to calculate how we would decline any forthcoming offer to pedal with us. Billy looked as if he had been pedaling for months in the same cut off Levi jeans and T-shirt. His once white high-top sneakers bore the grime and road grit of a thousand miles. I couldn't tell if his rail thin body and sun seared face was 25 years old or 55 years old. His disheveled long brown hair was pulled back in a ponytail bound with what looked like a tie made with an old clingy Saran wrap that once covered a tasty mustard and cheese gas station sandwich. He had an unexpectedly strong and fierce looking nose and cheek bones from which hung a shaggy blonde beard and mustache. The soil, winds and sun of the grasslands were etched on every exposed skin surface – yet he was full of energy and eager to share his story.

"I'm making this big bike ride to Akron, Ohio as a publicity stunt," said Billy. "You see I'm an inventor, and I'm going to sell my invention to B.F. Goodrich."

"Wow that's cool. What is your invention if we can ask?"

"Sure! It's a rubber combination tent-boat," he proudly stated.

"Is that what you have loading down your bike?"

"No, not really. See I haven't actually made my invention yet," Billy replied with undeterred confidence and honesty. "They don't know I'm coming to see Mr. Goodrich yet, but they will when the TV and newspapers pick up my story."

He went on to detail how his inflatable tent-boat would appeal to millions of campers and fishermen. We could do little but nod our heads in agreement. Then he saved us the embarrassment of having to make up a lie about why we couldn't ride along with him to Akron when he mercifully said,

"Well, I think I might just set up camp here by these shade trees. You fellas have a good ride. I hope you get to where you're going!"

"You too, Billy. Good luck", and we pulled out of the roadside rest with smiles on our faces and wishing we could be flies on the wall when Billy walked into the B.F. Goodrich corporate headquarters and asked to see the boss.

It was funny at the time, but after decades of practicing medicine I have seen a lot of Billys, and it is not funny. We don't often engage with people like Billy because they make us feel uncomfortable and ill-equipped to handle the interaction. They scare us. Will they ask me for money? Will they pull out a knife and kill me? I'm guessing Billy had some kind of mental impairment or type of bipolar disorder. He had no needle tracks, and drug addicts typically don't have the physical stamina Billy displayed with his open road pedaling of that Conestoga-like bike of his. Billy had a big dream, and he was taking real life action to accomplish it. In a way, it was admirable. Was it too different from me having a big dream? He wasn't hurting anybody, and who could say he was harming himself.

The issue with folks like Billy is that they can't see all the steps and reality needed to accomplish their big dream, and they get lost in it. Psychiatry then diagnoses them as delusional. When they are unable to accomplish their dream, they often decompensate, fall into severe despair or unsafe behaviors. That's when I met patients like Billy in the Emergency Room, injured or psychotic, often accompanied by a worried exhausted family. A couple of nights in the hospital with IV rehydration and loaded with the antipsychotic drug of the year would usually bring back the Billys to their more stable selves. The challenge with our treatment plans was finding a social setting where Billys could thrive, and a med dose that didn't eliminate the sparkle in their eyes and the joy, confidence, and hopefulness of a guy shouting "Hey fellas! I'm Billy".

I'm glad we met Billy when he was happy and pedaling toward his big dream – just like us. I hoped he got where he was going.

Chapter 18

Brotherhood and Pedaling Home Without Dick

Day 34 August 6

Terre Haute, Indiana to Lawrence, Indiana: 85 miles

Day 35 August 7

Lawrence, Indiana to New Paris, Ohio: 90 miles

Day 36 August 8

New Paris, Ohio to East Columbus, Ohio: 105 miles

Day 35 began waking up on a couch at the Indiana State University ΣAE (Sigma Alpha Epsilon) fraternity house. When we first wheeled up to the stately fraternity house and I was in awe. It appeared to be an old mansion with a finely groomed lawn and landscaping. Certainly, unlike my small Bethany College where most Greeks lived in 2 story college owned buildings with four suites of 4 rooms and a common area on each floor. Only four Greek organizations owned their own houses in town. Independent upperclassmen housing was very scarce, and many of the students (including me) joined fraternities and sororities for a decent place to live among other reasons. The ISU chapter was huge with just over 100 brothers. A few were hanging out on the porch and greeted us suspiciously as we rolled our bikes across the lawn.

"Hey, can we help you guys?" said the tall blonde sporting cut off jean shorts and flip flops as he jutted out his chest in a show of bravado.

"Hi ! We're biking cross country, and I am an ΣAE brother from West Virginia. I was hoping we could spend the night here. Wahda ya say?"

"I don't know man. How can we be sure you really are an ΣAE?" he replied.

What followed was a barrage of questions about ΣAE history. I was the 'Pledge Master' the year before and remembered all those worthless tidbits except I could not recall the names of all "Ten Founding Fathers".

"Come on dude, give me a break. I've been pedaling this bike for the past month and I'm lucky that I remember my name after today's hundred-mile ride in this heat."

"He did way better than I could have," the curly headed guy chimed in as he woke up from his afternoon beer nap on the chaise lounge chair.

With the correct secret handshake we were finally permitted entrance, offered a few brews, some food, and a place to sleep. We were much more laid back at Bethany College and I consider my years there as among my most amazing times of growth, friendship, and fun.

The Indiana State University ΣAE chapter still exists in 2024, but many chapters do not. Unfortunately, my ΣAE fraternity chapter was expelled from campus in 1983 for alleged drug activities. Even worse, nationwide several ΣAE fraternity chapters were involved in nine hazing, alcohol, and drug related deaths between 2006 and 2019. Multiple closures, suspensions, and legal actions rightfully occurred. This was a sad era for the victims, their families, and for the reputation of Greek fraternities in general. It serves as a reminder of what senseless actions can occur when entitled young men condone dangerous group behavior in the name of brotherhood. Extreme political groups and domestic terrorist groups feed off the same phenomenon. ProudBoys, Oath Keepers, and Three Percenters come to mind in 2024.

In an effort to restore some purpose and integrity to the national brand, ΣAE founded a leadership education program, became the first Greek fraternity to eliminate 'pledging', and banned 'hard alcohol' from fraternity events and activities. Too bad they didn't include hard drugs in that directive.

I am glad that my 1974 chapter was a diverse group of guys who engaged in no physical hazing or forced drinking rituals. This is not to say that beer didn't flow like a river on weekends while the aroma of pot wafted from many rooms. There were brother bike enthusiasts like my roommate Mike Sieber (aka The Kid), upperclassman John Majors and Ed Movic (aka Fast Eddy) who went on to make their own epic bike journeys. I made lasting friendships and was able to thrive in my "cube" of mostly pre-something students. The frat depended upon us to keep the average GPA above the suspension threshold. Always good to keep a few athletic nerds around.

An invitation to stay at the Indiana State University ΣAE house was way harder to obtain than the ΚΣ (Kappa Sigma) house that Bob found when we rolled into Topeka, Kansas four days earlier. All he had to do was ask if we could join them in their raucous outdoor spaghetti and beer party. One 'hell yeah' was the limit of their inquisition. Unfortunately, their fraternity house had to be torn down in 2015 as they were unable to afford its upkeep. I wonder if the beer and party budget became problematic.

The route from Terre Haute, Indiana, to Lawrence, Indiana, took us through the streets of Indianapolis, where I had to change the roll of film in my camera. I recall realizing that I had mostly been taking pictures of scenic vistas, state welcoming signs, and monuments like the Gateway Arch in St. Louis, Missouri and the Soldiers and the Sailors Monument in Indianapolis, Indiana. Why do I have no photos of the generous hosts who took us in along the way or the amazing and sometimes weird people we met? I wish I had taken a college course in photojournalism instead of photosynthesis.

I wrote in my journal, "Why have I never taken a picture of the whites and blacks in the ghetto areas, or their homes, or their streets? I think they will be remembered more than these monuments." Certainly, people and characters are more critical to a story than landscape and scenery. I didn't appreciate this obvious gap in capturing the memories of our journey; however, I was right about one thing. I do remember details about the people far more easily than details of the monuments.

Last mail stop was Lynn, Indiana. With shoes and gloves off we indulged in mailed candies, foil wrapped chocolate chip cookies, and letters from friends and home.

Debatably, the most memorable person from the summer of 1974 was Richard (Dick) Milhous Nixon. Full disclosure, I voted for George McGovern, his unsuccessful presidential challenger in 1972. Inflation was at 11.1%, and the national speed limit was lowered to 55 mph to conserve a looming gas shortage, which likely contributed to Nixon's low approval rating at the time. I was just tired of listening to Nixon denying involvement or knowledge of the Watergate Burglary[14], and to his Vice President Spiro Agnew denying allegations of fraud, bribery, and tax evasion. In October 1973 Agnew had finally caved in to the weight of mounting evidence and pleaded guilty to the lesser charge of tax evasion to avoid trial on the more serious charges. He voluntarily resigned and was replaced by House Minority Leader Gerald Ford. I was happy to be on a bike all day and away from the morning and evening TV news (no 24-hour news channels existed then). I was more concerned with the marble-sized hailstorm we rode into at the Indiana-Ohio state line.

We were cold and pelted with ice, so the motel in New Paris, Ohio, looked like a no brainer on that evening of August 7th. It was our only night in a hotel except for San Francisco.

The evening TV news reported that the Supreme Court had demanded the release of Nixon's secret White House tapes. The whole country could hear him cuss and discuss Watergate in no uncertain terms. He could no longer deny knowledge of the 1972 Watergate burglary attempt on the Democratic National Headquarters.

"Yeah, I thought he knew," said Bob.

"Will be interesting to see what happens next. We have about 100 miles to Mr. Fitzpatrick's house in Columbus. I guess we'll find out more then," I replied, having no idea of what was about to happen.

Had MSNBC or FOX been around in 1974, I would have been saturated in reporting on the 25th Amendment to the Constitution, and the impeachment process. Notably there were no legislators calling the tapes “fake” or “rigged” as there certainly would have been had this happened in 2024. Somehow the truth seemed easier for politicians to decern in 1974 as compared to 2024.

My father (aka Pop) was a staunch Republican and loved Dick Nixon. He defended Nixon’s ending the draft and opening relations with China, while I railed against his “tricky Dick” ethical shortcomings like a know-it-all college kid. Pop took over the family plumbing and heating business that my grandfather Lou W. Nau started in an old livery barn in 1920. In 1974 Pop started expanding the business into retail home improvement and plumbing supplies with a company called Nationaline in Columbus, Ohio. A Mr. Bill Fitzpatrick was the manager assigned to help with the launch. He and my father became close friends, and it was at his East Columbus home that Bob and I witnessed history.

On August 8, 1974, we sat around a black and white TV set and watched Walter Cronkite on the CBS Evening News cover Nixon's live resignation speech. The following day Vice President Gerald Ford would succeed him. Ford went on to lose the next election and became the only President of the United States of America that never won the general or electoral college vote for the position. Nixon cursorily apologized for making mistakes, and losing the support of Congress, without mentioning the impeachment proceedings which were about to commence. He recounted his accomplishments in office and a long Teddy Roosevelt quote about a man who "…spends himself in a worthy cause…at least fails while daring greatly."

I journaled "I'm glad to be living in a country where Nixon can get out with his life. We ought to give Dick an island, just like Napolean, and let him think things over while he writes his biography. Let's give him the respect of being a person, but not a president."

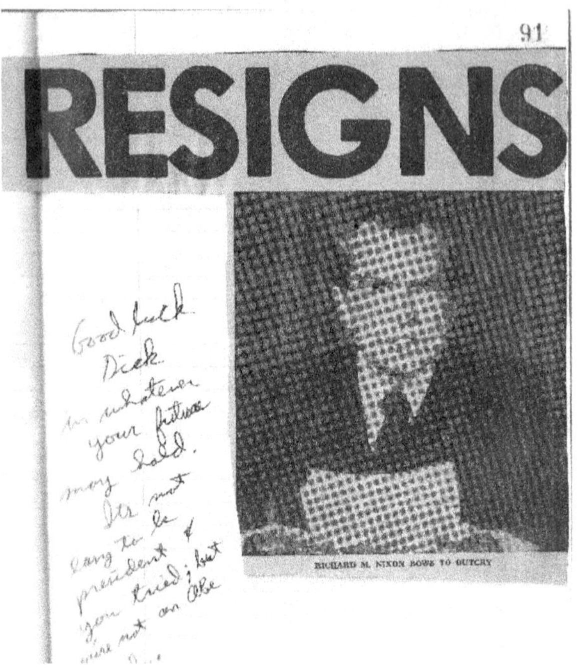
91

RESIGNS

RICHARD M. NIXON BOWS TO OUTCRY

Good luck
Dick
in whatever
your future
may hold.
Its not
easy to be
president &
you tried; but
you
were not an Abe

He lived out the remaining 20 years of his life in his La Casa Pacifica home in San Clemente, California, on a pension of $200,000 a year – hardly a Napoleonic Elba Island exile.

At least we didn't "have Dick Nixon to kick around anymore" (his own words) as we pedaled onward toward West Virginia.

Chapter 19

You Can Always Go Home

Day 37 August 9

East Columbus, Ohio to Piedmont, Ohio: 110 miles

Day 38 August 10

Piedmont, Ohio to Wheeling, West Virginia: 40 miles

Day 39-40 August 11-12

Wheeling, West Virginia: 0 miles

It took us two days to cover the 150 miles between East Columbus, Ohio, and our homes in Wheeling, West Virginia, where we would reunite with family and resupply. The Lewis and Clark Expedition floated down the Ohio from Pittsburgh, Pennsylvania, also stopped in Wheeling to pick up supplies - and a doctor. Unluckily, young Dr William E. Patterson missed the 3 PM departure time and they left without him. Fifty years ago, I never really thought about the origins of my hometown Wheeling's name. I assumed that it had to do settler wagon trains 'wheeling' down National Road as they headed westward. Somehow the Catholic nuns and brothers neglected to teach us that Wheeling was named by the Delaware Indians who called it *wih-link* -"place of the skull". It seems that some unwanted early pioneers had their heads removed from their bodies, placed atop wooden poles and displayed along the banks of the Ohio River to ward off outsiders. Evidently, this bit of dissident history uncomfortably conflicted with our town motto 'Wheeling-the Friendly City' and was omitted from our West Virginia History class.

Before you jump to conclusions and judge the

barbarity of our indigenous Wheelingites, don't forget that in 1661 England's King Charles II ordered the body of Oliver Cromwell exhumed and decapitated. He placed the head upon a 20-foot pole atop Westminster Hall to send a warning to anyone who would dare to threaten the monarchy. Cromwell earned the ire of King Charles II by overthrowing his father King Charles I and ruling England as its 'Lord Protector' for five monarch-free years. His head remained atop that pole for 23 years until it was blown off in a storm. A sentry is said to have found Olivers noggin, and this began nearly a century of the head being bought and sold by private citizens for their private museums. Finally, in 1960 Cromwell's head was properly buried at Sidney Sussex College, his alma mater. I wonder if this was perhaps a warning to alumni who dare to ignore donation requests.

Evidence of this unexplainable urge for homo sapiens to decapitate their enemies and display their heads on poles has been found in the Americas, Europe,

Asia and Africa – yet we call ourselves the evolved species. Fortunately, on August 10, 1974, we were free from the burden of the unsavory *wih-link* bit of history, and we prepared to pedal into our Friendly City without fear or trepidation. We were close to home.

Our last night before parading into Wheeling was spent at a campground in Piedmont, Ohio. Nearby Piedmont Lake was the site of my disappointing high school 'night after prom' where my last-minute date and I along with another couple 'slept' in a station wagon after an all-night bowling alley party. Sadly, there was no memorable skinny dipping or loss of virginity. The Jesuit brothers running Central Catholic High School probably prayed for the cold and rainy weather that left us cramped and confined to the car. Oh well, another sexless night in Piedmont, Ohio, would not dampen my anticipated victorious bicycle home all the way from San Francisco.

It was a hot and sticky morning as we pedaled

across the Wheeling Suspension Bridge. We stopped and posed for a photo on this 1,010-foot steel structure which was the first to span a major river on the National Road (now Route 40). For two years in the mid-1800s it was the largest suspension bridge in the world; however, the bridge closed to vehicular traffic in 2019 and in 2024 is only traveled by pedestrians and bicyclists.

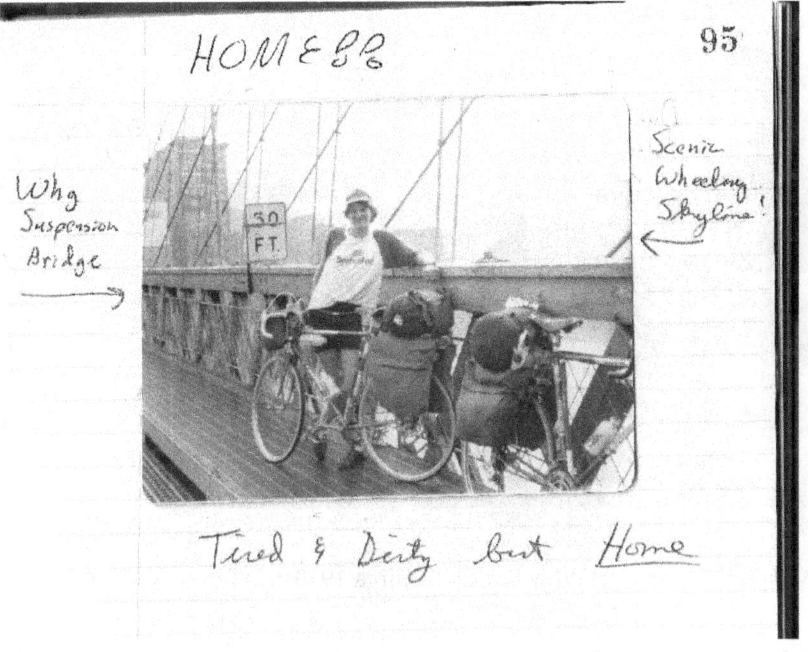

Page 95 of my journal

In the photo I am sporting a sun visor, and my cotton

baseball-style shirt with a 10-speed bike decal and the words 'Deutschland' printed across the front. This was my 'back-up' shirt when not wearing my nylon blend official bicycling shirt with rear pockets. Although proud of my Teutonic heritage, I think I wore that 'Deutschland' shirt more to lure geographically challenged but beautiful girls to ask me if I was bicycling from Germany. It didn't work.

Mingo Stature atop Wheeling Hill. Circa 1930s

We followed National Road up the short steep west side of Wheeling Hill. Atop the promontory the 'Mingo Statue' welcomed us home. This tall bronze statue of a

Mingo Indian brave stood with outstretched right arm and the inscription "The MINGO, original inhabitants of this Valley, extends GREETINGS and PEACE to all Wayfarers." There was no plaque describing how the Mingo, part of the Iroquois Federation, were driven from Wheeling in the 1800s. After being forced into Ohio, most indigenous people were relocated to Kansas and eventually to Oklahoma under the Indian Removal Act of 1830. In 1982 three men from Columbus, Ohio cut off the Mingo statue at the ankles and stole it. They were betrayed by an anonymous tipster that I hope was a Native American. The next year the recovered statue was reunited with its' feet and restored to its original base.

Within a hundred yards we then passed McColloch's Leap plaque. In 1777 Major Samuel McCulloch found himself outside of Wheeling's Fort Henry as the gate was closed during an unexpected Indian attack. McCulloch headed up Wheeling Hill to escape the warriors but encountered another war party.

Knowing that his reputation preceded him, and fearing a slow tortuous death, he spurred his horse over the edge of a 300-foot precipice into the creek below. History has it that the Indians expected to see his dead body when they peered over the cliffside, but instead saw McCulloch galloping away on his white horse. This made him even more infamous, so his heart was removed from his body and eaten by the Indians who finally caught up with him in 1782 – proving that fame can have its drawbacks. After passing these commemorations to the Indigenous people that were driven away, and the soldier that leaped away, we paused and looked at each other.

"Let's go!", I said.

"Onward to home!", declared Bob, and we pedaled, tucked and raced down the long east slope of Wheeling Hill.

One mile later, at the top of Chicken Neck Hill, Bob peeled off to his home on Maple Avenue and I continued another half mile taking a right at the corner where the family plumbing/heating and now home improvement store stood. We gave our families a call from a pay phone in downtown Wheeling, so they were expecting us. I arrived at our red brick home on tree lined Locust Avenue with a front porch "Welcome Home KC" sign created by my little sisters. My mom was teary and gave me a big kiss. Pop was still at work and would return for dinner as usual at 5:00 pm. Times of reunion with both parents and all seven of us kids would become less frequent over the next 50 years, but never less precious than in 1974.

After several years of infertility, my mother bore seven children within 10 years. She was either pregnant or holding a baby in most of my childhood memories. My parents, Dick and Jane, were everything to us children. In first grade I was certain that our reader Dick and Jane was about them. 'See Dick run. See Jane run. Run, Dick, run. Run, Jane, run.' Eventually Mom told me that the books were not about them, and later I realized that Dick and Jane were brother and sister. Nonetheless, they were still famous in my eyes.

Mom's blood type was Rh negative and all seven of us kids were Rh positive. This was before the development of RhoGam - an antibody injection routinely given to Rh negative mothers to prevent their blood from attacking the blood of their Rh-positive fetuses. My sister Jennifer (Nau child #7) required a total exchange blood transfusion because of the Rh incompatibility. She turned ten in 1974 and did everything with my sister Megan (Nau child #6).

Megan was a little over 1 year older than Jennifer. She recalls crying when Pop and I left for the Pittsburgh train station at night and helping to make the welcome home sign. I remember her as the more mischievous of the two littlest sibs, and that they both got away with murder after we older siblings left the nest.

My sister, and future schoolteacher, Gretchen (Nau child #5) was 14 years old and recalled parental updates on our trip progress after they received post cards, letters or phone calls. She was the family artist and orchestrated the Welcome Home sign. She wondered why I got to bike cross country while she was "bored" and had only been out of West Virginia twice.

My sister Tama (Nau child #2) was pursuing her Dental Hygiene degree at West Liberty State College. I was one of her 'volunteer patients' in 1974. She was dating her future husband Jim, a bit of a renegade guy who we sibs all loved, but who took some time to earn the affection of my father.

My brother Matt (Nau child #4) was an avid biker, pedaling all around Wheeling on a ten-speed bike (purchased from our Anybody's Bike Shop) and working as a grass cutter at the local cemetery. We are 4 years apart and still reunite for long distance bicycle adventures including Ride the Rockies in Colorado and Cycle Oregon events.

My brother Jeff (Nau child #3) was working at the

plumbing shop and preparing to start at Fairmont State College on a swimming scholarship where he would earn his AA degree in Retail Management. Our grandfather, Lou W Nau, started the plumbing shop at the corner of Edgington Lane and National Road in 1920. My father, Richard Louis Nau, assumed leadership in 1952. Jeff took over the family business in 1988 and retired in 2024 – the last plumber at Lou W. Nau, Inc.

Circa 1954

Circa 2024

Jeff's children Justin Nau and Heather Gilot are the fourth Nau generation operating what is now exclusively a home improvement and hardware store. My father's 1974 foresight to venture into this retail sector has come full circle in 2024 to perpetuate the family business. My brothers and sisters are important to me now more than ever. Pop died from a stroke in 2000, and my mother recently died from Alzheimer's Dementia at age 94. For the first time in my life, I have no parental 'home' to return to. Mom's home was sold to settle the estate. We seven children had a very spirited and civil (fueled by beer and wine) round-robin claiming of mom's belongings. She would have been amused. After her funeral we 7 children, and most of mom's 18 grandchildren and her 19 great-grandchildren had a big party at her house. We invited all to take home any little remaining family treasures. Nearly everyone had something that reminded them of visiting mom, something small and often unnoticed by the rest. In 2024 the house where we seven grew up on Locust Avenue sits vacant and falling in disrepair due to the insane negligence of the current owner. The last house my parents lived together until Pop died sits tall and well-kept high on the creek bank, but the wheelchair ramp we built for Pop after his stroke is gone. Now the garden condominium unit on Elm Street where mom lived for her final 22 years is no longer our 'home'.

Does it seem silly that her son, old enough for Medicare, could miss the warm embrace of that apartment, mom and her furnishings and seasonal nicknacks that we all grew up with? So, now my coming 'home' is mostly seeing my brothers and sisters at family reunions and weddings where we all sit back and realize that we are now the "old people" at these events. I think we all secretly pray that we are as loved and cherished by our children and grandchildren as Mom and Pop were by us.

L to R : Standing- Matt, me, Jeff. Sitting-Megan, Jennifer, Tama, Gretchen. (Circa 1975)

Mom's 90th Birthday Party (L to R) Back Row: Gretchen, Tama, Jennifer, Megan, me. Front Row: Jeff, Mom, Matt. (July 14, 2019)

Bob's homecoming was equally heartwarming and uplifting for him. His father had died of heart problems in 1973 at the age of 50. Mr. Gantzer ran the IBM computer at Wheeling Machine Products, as well as side jobs bookkeeping for a bakery, and establishing a family business of making rubber stamps. Bob and his siblings all learned to make stamps and received an education in business as well as some spending money in return. Despite being a 48-year-old widowed mother of six children, Bob's mom continued to encourage him to take the bike journey. She was always kind and upbeat when we would sit on their front porch after Bob and I finished a training ride.

(L to R) Judy, Susan, Chris, Bob's Mom Helen, Bob, Jay, and Dave Gantzer (Circa 1978)

Bob had two older sisters, Chris (the smart, responsible 26-year-old mother of two), and Susan (the ornery 23-year-old nurse), and a younger sister Judy (15 years old that summer and in charge of keeping Bob's tropical fish alive).

Dave was Bob's analytical 20-year-old brother who wrote in a letter to Bob that summer "this trip is one in a lifetime experience and a lot of pictures will come in handy when you and KC get back together 50 years from now to reminisce…who knows you might write a book about your experience." Little did he know that Bob had abandoned his journal writing 2 weeks into the trip, but he did take a lot of pictures.

His free-spirited younger brother, Jay, was 17 years old and worked at Burger Chef where he learned how to properly cut tomatoes and pocket a stack of redeemed free meal coupons for us. Bob and I never talked about the impact of his father's death or how it felt to become the oldest man in the house. The subject just never came up and male bonding with shared 'feelings' wasn't really a thing in 1974. What was obvious to me, however, was how intently Bob read those letters from home and how proud his mom was of her eldest son.

Our loving families would have understood and supported us if we had called it quits in Wheeling – but we would have forever wondered why we never made it to Ocean City. Country singer/songwriter Alan Jackson has a song You Can Always Come Home[15]

"You can always come home.

So, pack your bags, smile and say goodbye

And chase those dreams"

On Day 41, August 13, 1974, we saddled up and pedaled off to finish what we started. The local newspaper ran a front-page article on us titled 'Trip Hasn't Been All Downhill for Cyclists'. We were better hydrated, fed, and rested than we had ever been in the last 2 months. There could be no turning back now.

Trip Hasn't Been All Downhill for Cyclists

By ANDY LEDENY
The Intelligencer Staff

It's safe to say that K.C. Nau and Bob Gantzer of Wheeling enjoy bicycle riding.

Between July 4 and Aug. 10, they've traveled more than 3,170 miles on bicycles.

Nau, a resident of 7 Locust Ave., and Gantzer, of 105 Maple Ave., have wanted to make a cross-country bicycle trip for the last two years. This summer they are making it a reality.

Nau and Gantzer stopped in Wheeling Saturday to visit their families as their journey neared its close. They will leave Wheeling today and hope to arrive at Ocean City, Md. by Monday.

"The urge to make a cross-country bike trip began when we made a trip to the Atlantic Coast two years ago," Gantzer said. "The difference in terrain between the beach and the Wheeling area really intrigued us. We thought it would be exciting to see the differences in appearances in all parts of the country.

"Our trip began June 30," Nau said. "That's when we boarded a train in Pittsburgh for San Francisco.

"We wanted to start our trip on the west coast," the 20-year-old senior at Bethany College continued. "If you're going to make a cross country journey by bike, it's best to travel from west to east. By traveling this way, you take better advantage of prevailing winds."

Nau said an official of the League of American Wheelmen secured a travel route map for the trip. He said the hardest part of the journey was the first week when the pair had to travel over mountainous terrain.

"But as for the physical aspect of the journey," Gantzer, a 21-year-old senior at Wheeling College, said, "it's not as tiring as one would think. After your legs get used to it, the action of bicycling doesn't bother you at all."

Nau said he and Gantzer originally intended to travel about 60 miles per day, but have actually averaged thus far 75 miles per day.

The bicyclists said their expenses were budgeted to no more than $5 per day. However, the pair suffered a setback in Tonopah, Nev., when 100 ball bearings fell out of the gear cluster of Nau's vehicle.

"From that point on, we could only spend $3 a day," Nau said. "We needed the other money to repair the bike."

The Wheeling residents said probably the most interesting aspect of their journey thus far has been the people they have met.

"What sticks uppermost in my mind [illegible] now," Nau said, "is our journey [illegible] the desert. It's impossible to [illegible] how hot it is.

"[illegible] one night of camping out in the [illegible]," he said, "we saw some wild [illegible]. We didn't think much about it [illegible] middle of the night. That's when [illegible] horses stampeded our camp. [illegible] our bikes and equipment were [illegible]," he said.

[illegible] their journey just over a month [illegible] pair have traveled through 10 [illegible] and used seven spare tires in the [illegible]. Neither feels the journey has [illegible] particularly grueling. Both believe the [illegible] has been rewarding.

"[illegible] trip has taught me one important [illegible]," Nau said, "that Wheeling has a lot [illegible] young people than I ever [illegible]. Most of the communities we [illegible] through did not have the parks [illegible] opportunities for enjoyment [illegible] Wheeling has for both young and [illegible].

"[illegible] one reason why I would [illegible] a similar trip for anyone," [illegible] said. "You can learn a great deal [illegible].

"[illegible] there's just no better way to see the [illegible] States."

Heading to Finish

All set to complete their cross-country bike trip are Wheeling residents K. C. Na[illegible] left, and Bob Gantzer. The cyclists have traveled approximately 3,170 miles thus [illegible]
(Photo by Lebeu

Chapter 20

Appalachians and Appaloosas

Day 41 August 13

Wheeling, West Virginia to Morgantown, WV: 85 miles

Day 42 August 14

Morgantown, West Virginia: 0 miles

Day 43 August 15

Morgantown, WV to Spring Gap, Maryland: 90 miles

Day 44 August 16

Spring Gap, Maryland to Indian Spring, Maryland: 55 miles

Day 45 August 17

Indian Spring, Maryland to Alexandria, Virginia: 108 miles

Our final mountain range to conquer was the

Appalachians. This string of alternating ridgelines and valleys stretches from the Island of Newfoundland, Canada, to the state of Alabama. This geographical fact is often overlooked by many whose minds immediately zero in on banjo players with bad teeth in the deep hollers of Kentucky and Georgia.

Older than the Rocky Mountains, the Appalachian Mountains have undergone 240 million years of weathering and the peaks we would pedal over along our route through West Virginia, Pennsylvania and Maryland were only in the 3,000-foot elevation range. Broadleaf trees with spectacular fall foliage are dominant as opposed to the evergreens out west. The oaks and maples were home to many more birds than we ever saw or heard out west. Squirrels and chipmunks frequently raced across the road inches ahead of us. Less fortunate opossums that couldn't outrun a truck occasionally adorned the white line with their four legs pointing skyward and emitting various degrees of roadkill aroma. The Appalachian peaks, although puny by Coloradoite standards, possessed the great equalizers of high humidity, grades often steeper than the average 6% grades of Colorado mountain passes, and nearly nonexistent pavement to the right of the white line. The final six days were no ride in the park.

"Let's detour over to Morgantown and visit Bookstore Bobby," I suggested to Bob as we pedaled east on National Road.

"Sounds good to me. You can actually legally drink beer there," replied Bob with a smile.

He was eager to maintain our beer in every state streak and to remind me that he had to sneak me beer in a few 21 and over states. We powered over hill after hill and covered the 85 miles to Morgantown, West Virginia, by late afternoon. It took us two hours to find our friend's apartment just off the sprawling campus of West Virginia University.

In 1974 I could only dream of attending medical

school there. I would have declared you high on some illegal substance if you had told me that I would become a WVU Professor of Family Medicine and Dean of the Eastern Division Regional Campus of the WVU School of Medicine. Like most 20-year-olds, I only dared to envision the future 1-4 years away.

Bob (our friend whose home housed our bike shop back home) was working his way through college as night janitor at the hospital that summer. He did not get off till midnight, so we spent the time drinking famous 'fishbowls' at a bar called Marios. These huge chalices of cold frosted glass held about a quart of West Virginia's regulated 3% beer. What it lacked in fish or alcohol was compensated for in volume. Many a Mario Fishbowl has been hoisted high to celebrate a Mountaineer football victory after joining the whole stadium in singing Country Roads. I still get chills thinking about singing that song.

After we reassembled at the apartment, we

cooked all the food in his refrigerator into the wee hours of the morning and shared stories with Bookstore. It was supposed to have been the three of us completing this epic journey, but he never seemed to wallow in his disappointment of being unable to go. That was the last time I spent any time in person with one of my closest teenage friends. He went on to work for the Public Health Department in Charleston, West Virginia, and later became a lawyer. He was always incredibly smart, and I am sure he was a great attorney to have on your side. Despite paying for several 'we can locate anyone' websites, I was unable to reach him at any of the phone numbers or addresses that were offered. I am sorry that I failed to keep in contact with him periodically over these past 50 years.

Day 43 was a cloudless, searingly hot day. The coolest thing was pedaling in three separate states in one day – West Virginia, Pennsylvania, and Maryland. I looked shockingly pale in my shirtless photo poses at each state's WELCOME sign, except for my forearms and lower legs. We pumped over Maryland's Mount Savage and soared down the eastern face toward the promise of reaching Cumberland and the Chesapeake & Ohio (C&O) Canal. On paper the towpath looked like a 180-mile gradual downhill route allowing us to coast into the nation's capital. The C&O Canal was originally George Washington's idea to connect inland America with the Atlantic Ocean via the Chesapeake Bay. Thomas Jefferson envisioned that multiple canals would eventually connect the Great Lakes with the Ohio River. Mules harnessed to canal boats and barges by ropes would pull the vessels as they walked along the towpaths adjacent to the canals.

C&O Canal construction began in 1828 but took an agonizing twenty-two years to complete, and never made it to the Ohio River. A series of 74 locks would enable travel up and down the C&O Canal, bypassing the rapids of the parallel Potomac River. Lock operators would live in lock houses, many of which still stand and are restored for rustic lodging by the C&O Canal Trust.

Lock construction around formidable rapids at Harpers Ferry, West Virginia, Seneca, Maryland, and Great Falls, Virginia, took longer than expected and were considered engineering feats. The one-mile-long tunnel, an engineering obstacle required at Paw Paw, West Virginia, to bypass five Potomac River bends, took fourteen years to complete. Finally, by 1850 coal, lumber, and farm produce were able to be transported from Cumberland, Maryland, to Washington DC by canal barges.

Boat on C&O Canal – towpath on right. Circa 1900-1924.

As with many technologies, canal transport had a shortened lifespan due to the success of the emerging railroad system which provided a less expensive and faster mode of transportation. A powerful Potomac River flood in 1924 damaged much of the canal beyond repair and it slowly suffered from the forces of abandonment and erosion. In 1954, the year of my birth, bureaucrats declared the C&O Canal "devoid of commercial or scenic value" and proposed a new automobile highway be built atop the canal and towpath. When Congress approved the project Supreme Court Justice William O Douglass leaped into action to save the canal. This robust Justice, originally from Yakima, Washington, was an outdoor and conservation enthusiast known for hiking with a twenty-pound pack to strengthen himself from the lingering effects of polio. The C&O Canal Towpath provided him with a gateway to nature right there in Washington, DC. He organized and led a 185-mile C&O Canal hike to raise public awareness of Congress's environmentally evil plan. His persistent grassroots efforts finally led to Congress declaring the canal a National Park in 1971 to be restored for hiking, biking and horseback riding.

Over the years the National Park Service has restored the Paw Paw Tunnel and covered the towpath with fine crushed limestone, but in 1974 the park was only 3 years into this project. Due to repeated rockfalls, the Paw Paw Tunnel was closed so we eagerly joined up with the towpath at Spring Gap, Maryland, at mile marker 173. To say that we found the towpath was not yet 'restored' would be an understatement. I'm pretty sure that I pedaled over wagon wheel ruts and petrified mule poop from the 1800's. It briefly rained and our narrow bike tires easily sank into the wet surface.

"Bob, this sucks", I declared wiping splattered mud from my leg.

"Let's get off this thing. I'd rather bike up mountains than plow through this," said Bob.

So, at Little Orleans, Maryland, we left the banks of the Potomac River and looked for a backroad that would lead us to Route 40. This decision proved to have fatal implications for our dream of pedaling into Ocean City. We headed up the coarse asphalt of High Germany Road to Little Orleans – a one building town. Bill's Place (a combination restaurant/bar) was closed - an ominous sign.

In 2024 the town's population of 42 anticipates the 21st Annual Apple's East Coast Sturgis Rally. Whereas the famous South Dakota Sturgis Rally attracts almost half a million Harley-Davison lovers, this backwoods Maryland event can only accommodate about 10,000 bikers. Every August, about the same time we passed through, motorcycle enthusiasts now gather on nearby Apple Mountain. The event proudly hosts music, lady wrestling, a motorcycle demolition derby and "is not a place where you have to watch every move you make". Outside firewood and chainsaws are, however, strictly prohibited. Promoters advertise that you can camp for the single price of $100 in either your RV, your tent or "passed out on the ground". Lamentably, we were 39 years too early for East Coast Sturgis and on the wrong 2 wheeled vehicles.

The road out of the Potomac riverbanks over Apple Mountain included two areas with Mount Everest-like grades. I had to practically jump on each pedal every inch of the slow way up. The strain on my rear wheel was palpable, like the thin ice just before the cracks started as we walked on newly frozen Wheeling Creek as kids. Near the crest the dreaded 'PING' of a broken spoke suddenly echoed up the hollow. This was followed by a second 'TWANG' and the inevitable wheel-wobble against the caliper brake pads.

"Damit !" I shouted into the heavens, but only the circling buzzards and Bob could hear me.

Another roadside wheel truing and rear brake disabling allowed me to continue the sweaty ride in 90 degrees heat and 90 degrees humidity up Orleans Road to Route 40. We discovered that Old Route 40 shared the road with Interstate-70 for a few miles east of Hancock.

"Looks like we have to make another illegal ride on the Interstate again", I said after consulting our map and seeing no alternative.

Without a word or worry Bob took off onto the entrance ramp. I wondered if maybe we would be arrested and get to spend that night in jail that he was supposed to request back in Sedalia, Missouri. We put our heads down and pedaled like crazy till the Old Route 40 exit as the rain started on our approach to Indian Springs, Maryland. Once again providence provided us with none other than the Indian Springs General Store. We spent $3.50 each and cooked our Dinty Moore Beef Stew on the wide oak planked front porch. We sopped up the gravy with a half a loaf of bread and washed it all down with a Coke. A local farmer, Mitch, sat down on the wooden bench next to the Coke machine and shot the shit with us as we ate.

"So, the owner tells me you boys are biking across the USA," said Mitch, with a toothpick hanging out of the corner of his mouth and thumbs tucked into the pockets of his faded overalls.

"That's right, sir. We were happy to find this place and escape the rain," I replied.

“Well, my farm is just down the road and you boys are welcome to stay in my barn if you’d like” he offered.

“That would be great."

“I have a couple of horses in that barn, but they are in stalls all night."

“That’s no problem, we like horses”, I said having no idea how Bob felt about horses after the Nye County stampede. I could only envision sleeping in a bed of soft dry hay out of the approaching thunderstorm.

The horses were Appaloosas, and their big brown eyes followed us as we opened the heavy barn door with its fading red paint. A familiar "Chew Mail Pouch Tobacco, Treat Yourself to the Best" ad was painted on the barn side that faced the road. The Bloch Brothers Tobacco Company of Wheeling, West Virginia sponsored these iconic hand painted ads on over 20,000 barns in 22 states between 1891 and the 1970's. I never sampled this carcinogenic hometown product, but took a strange pride in seeing that ad. The horses munched their feed and casually watched us find a spot to lean our bikes and spread out our sleeping bags for the night. We wondered if horse saddles would be more comfortable than our bike saddles after 43 days.

I slid into my blue sleeping bag and passed out. Eight hours later I awoke to the sound of roosters and the smell of horse poop – a true Old MacDonald's farm morning. The stall doors were already open, allowing the horses to wander into the fenced yard where they ate fresh grass. One of these beautiful animals had chestnut spots on its white coat and the other black/gray spots.

Bob checking out an alternative saddle in Spring Gap, MD barn

Spotted horses have been around for a long time. They appear in Stone Age cave paintings in France. North American Appaloosa horses came from wild mustang herds that originated from those brought over by Spaniard explorers. The Nez Perce tribe bred Appaloosa mustangs and called them Palouse horses after the river of similar name in Idaho.

Up well before us, Mitch and his wife Doris had eggs, bacon, and toast on the table and invited us in for breakfast. They were our harbor in a storm, as once again, we had stumbled upon genuine kindness.

The following day we pedaled off to the warm goodbyes from Mitch and Doris and wound our way to Boonsboro, Maryland, then on to Harpers Ferry, West Virginia.

Harpers Ferry, WV. Potomac River in foreground, Shenandoah River on left

This was the location alleged to inspire the lyrics "Blue Ridge Mountains, Shenandoah River" in John

Denver's hit song Country Roads (the de facto state anthem of West Virginia). This cozy town nestled at the confluence of the Shenandoah River and the Potomac River is where I would one day practice medicine for 35 years. It is also where Dr Rosemarie Cannarella, MD and Dr Linda Shields, MD and I would establish the Harpers Ferry Rural Family Medicine Residency Program in 1994.

In 1974 Harpers Ferry was just another beautiful spot on the 108 miles from Indian Springs, Maryland to Alexandria, Virginia. My journal entry was very brief. "Great day! Made it to the DC area and stayed at Bob's friend's apartment. "

I have no idea why pasted to that page is a photo of the brick apartment's second story balcony with someone's yellow 10-speed bike and a beagle dog.

My photo-journalistic skills were clearly withering.

So too was my rear wheel.

Chapter 21

Deviantly Crossing the Finish Line

Day 46 August 17

Alexandria, VA to Ocean City, MD: 155 miles (100 by truck)

My younger son Mike and his family now live south of Alexandria, Virginia. During his career in the construction industry, he has custom built roofing and floor trusses to exacting engineering criteria. He understands the importance of design integrity and would have reminded me that bicycle wheels are designed to hold up to incredible forces - if all the spokes are present. Nonetheless, on Day 46 I trued my rear wheel, minus two spokes, as best as possible. I was about to fall victim to the Normalization of Deviancy.

Normalization of Deviancy is a term first coined by Diane Vaughn after researching the cause of the Space Shuttle Challenger disaster. The O-rings on the fuel tank of the Challenger were designed to contain the volatile hot gases released during takeoff and tested for integrity between 40 degrees and 90 degrees. Previous experience with these booster O-rings showed that they could perform well even outside of these temperatures, and the flight engineers became used to getting away with safe O-ring operations in low temperatures that deviated from the original range. This created a false sense of safety under unsafe conditions – thus the term Normalization of Deviancy. The temperature at the time of the 1986 Challenger takeoff was 22 degrees, the O-rings failed, and the shuttle exploded killing all 7 crew members aboard while millions of school children watched on live TV to see schoolteacher-astronaut Christa McAuliffe.

The results of my Normalization of Deviancy of course pale in comparison to this national tragedy, but the process was similar. I had normalized the deviant way that my rear wheel was surviving with two broken spokes. After pedaling 55 miles from Alexandria, Virginia, to Annapolis, Maryland, we were on Route 50 heading to the Chesapeake Bay Bridge.

"Oh noooooo…" I yelled.

Suddenly, my rear wheel buckled, throwing me to the ground. I laid there looking at my rear wheel. Five additional spokes snapped, and the wheel abruptly curved into the shape of a crescent moon. August 18, 1974, was a Sunday, and no bike shops would be open. We decided to try and hitch a ride into Annapolis and see if we could find a bike shop that would be open on Monday and then find a place to camp for the night. It took less than five minutes before a white pickup truck pulled over.

"Hey, where are you guys headed?" asked Dan through the hand cranked, rolled down passenger window.

"My rear wheel just died and we're looking for a ride to a bike shop in Annapolis. Then we're finishing our cross-country ride in Ocean City," I replied.

"No shit!" Dan exclaimed. I'm just driving back home to good old Ocean City from California. But hey, I have to tell you guys, you should not be pedaling on Rt 50. It's really dangerous, and besides, you can't bike across the Bay Bridge."

We and our map maker Clifford Franz were unaware of this small fact. The Chesapeake Bay Bridge (now called the Governor William Preston Lane Jr. Memorial Bridge) had an original 4-mile span that was the world's longest continuous over-water steel structure. In 1973, due to traffic demands, a parallel span was added. They had a clearance of 186 feet to accommodate ocean freight vessels, but neither had bicycle lanes nor sidewalks. This tall narrow structure has low guard rails and frequent high winds that made it one of the scariest bridges in the country. Drivers petrified by bridges (called gephyrophobia) could have bridge personnel drive them across the bridge. Dan did not think that they provided this service for bicyclists.

Chesapeake Bay Bridge

So, there we were, practically in the shadow of the Bay Bridge, talking to a guy we just met through an open pickup truck window, having to make a big decision.

"So, what's it gonna be guys?" asked Dan.

"Well Bob, what do you think?" I asked, with a smile, hoping we would be on the same page.

"I think these last few miles are going to be a bigger problem and with more traffic to contend with than it's probably worth", he replied with a corresponding grin.

My journal notes that "we were tired, anxious, and on the verge of ecstasy". Needless to say – we loaded up our bikes and hopped in the truck.

Memories flashed back to driving across the Bay Bridge and staring out at the water as I had in the third seat of our family station wagon as a kid. We three boys and some luggage got the cramped last row, which had facing seats, while three of my sisters got the second row, and my parents and youngest sister got the front seat. We got stuck in traffic for two hours once (before they built the second span) and mom got a sunburn so bad on her thighs and window-side arm that she spent the first two days of vacation inside our air-conditioned boardwalk rental unit covered with Noxzema Cold Cream.

There is something about big bodies of water that draws us humans to their shores. Something that possesses parents to endure the 10-hour ordeal of a car trip with seven kids. Something that possessed me to enter the Great Chesapeake Bay Bridge Swim thirteen years after crossing in a pickup truck with my disabled bike in the truck bed. Maybe I was trying to compensate for a bicycle crossing that never happened. Maybe I was trying to conquer the bridges and body of water that prevented us from pedaling over and on to Ocean City.

I did 'conquer' those four miles of water twice as a middle of the pack swimmer, once with my Fairmont State University Hall of Fame swimmer brother Jeff who finished first in his age group. My last attempt in 1991 proved that the Bay ultimately decides who makes it across. Seven hundred and twenty swimmers (including me, my brother Matt and my brother-in-law Jim) had to be pulled from the water because stronger than anticipated currents were forcing us out from between the bridges and out of the safety zone of Coast Guard monitoring. We had to be bussed back over the bridge – another disappointing crossing by a means other than that which I had started.

But in 1974, the disappointment of having to be driven over the Bay Bridge quickly faded away as we drank beer and shared cross-country journey stories as our savior Dan drove along (Maryland had no open-container law until 2002). He was also the electrician for the Birds Nest Campground – with campsites and a handful of small wooden two room bungalows on a bay inlet just outside of Ocean City.

"Hey Dan, do you think you could get us into one of these cabins?" I asked.

"They'll be so happy to see me back at work that I might even be able to get you a deal, if they have any available," replied Dan with the air of confidence that one gets with having traveled across the country and drinking beer.

Thankfully, he came through for us. Our cabin was more like a little red wooden fishing shack with a tiny screened in porch, but our unit on the water's edge of the back bay seemed like a 4-start resort to me. The musty mattresses, humid lack of air-conditioning, and occasional scamper of mice across the pine board floors could not dull my joy and relief. Before going to bed that night, I sat outside the cabin and savored the star filled eastern skies high above the distant glow of the boardwalk bustle.

Yet there was one last stretch of road to bicycle – the 3.2 miles from the Birds Nest to the shores of Ocean City. Bob's brother had driven his old yellow Pinto from Wheeling to the beach to retrieve us. He brought his bike along, so I switched out my damaged wheel

Our Birds Nest cabin with bikes loaded on Bob's brother Dave's car

with his perfectly round rear wheel. I was back on my bike.

We had not inhaled that unmistakable fresh and salty ocean air since July 4th as it blew in off the Pacific. Now the late summer ocean winds blew in off the Atlantic and filled the air.

"Can you believe we're finally here?" Bob shouted as we weaved in and out of vacationer traffic.

"Bob, I never doubted that we could make it, but I was never really sure that we would until today. This is great!" I proclaimed.

My 1974 Post Card of Ocean City, Maryland

The two of us pedaled triumphantly into Ocean City. Then with bikes locked to a boardwalk lamp post, we took off our shoes, jogged across the hot sand to the cool water's edge, and waded into the August Atlantic surf. We finally made it. There was no welcoming throng of tourists or reporters, and no parade or fanfare. Our front-page story from the Wheeling Intelligencer apparently did not get picked up on the Associated Press wire for national distribution.

****

No one knew of our arrival except for us and our families – and that was just fine. Our rewards were much more enduring than momentary kudos from strangers. We had accomplished something hard, overcome adversity, and developed new resiliency. We had endured desert sun, windstorms, pouring rain, mountain hail, and more flat tires than we ever imagined possible. We pedaled side by side, drafted each other for speed, sweated up mountains and raced down the other side. We created these and many more memories while cycling through the grandeur of our country.

Most memorable, however, was the total trust we placed in each other and in the kindness of strangers. We experienced soul renewing solitude, as well as a panoply of unforgettable people who brought out new conversational confidence in us. Their diversity opened my eyes to cultures within our country that this West Virginia boy had never before encountered. I felt the best of humanity.

I was fortunate to get accepted into medical school later that year, and to keep riding that bike through my career in medicine. The next fifty years I also rode that feeling from the summer of 1974, and tried to put something kind into the lives of others. So did Bob.

Me at Wolf Creek Pass, Colorado (July 23, 1974)

In retirement, I can see that my patients, colleagues, and students enriched my life in ways I could never imagine. They affirmed for me that poem hanging on the bicycle shop wall in Colorado; "What we put into the lives of others, comes back into our own." This was my enduring lesson as I pedaled from the Pacific Ocean to the Atlantic Ocean in the summer of 1974 - and that's what I'll tell my grandkids happened 50 years ago – when I rode a bike.

Afterword by Bob

Hi, this is Bob, KC's biking partner 50 years ago. Where has the time gone? Almost 2 years ago, KC reached out to me to say he was thinking of writing a book about our summer of 1974. To quote him 'with a 50-year perspective on how things/people/ourselves have changed or remained the same'. Now, almost 50 years to the date he tells me 'I have just about finished the book', and has invited me to pen an Afterward. So, this is my story of the last 50 years.

After we finished the trip, life started back so fast that I did not take time to think about the accomplishment of a completed trip. When returning home, almost immediately I was back to work at the A&P and back to college, leaving little time for evaluation. I knew it was a 'once in a lifetime' journey, I knew my family was proud of me and I knew that my friends envied the experience.

I cannot tell you how much the completion of the journey had on my life. It has never left me. I now know that anything could be done with proper planning and a targeted focus. I have had success in my personal and professional life that might not have happened if not for this trip. It changed my vision and opened many doors that I would not have seen in the past. I am very much an introverted individual. The trip allowed me to meet many people, not worry about where you are going to sleep tomorrow or think about if we have enough to eat, drink, money… . This experience matured me and helped develop my personality. I came out of my shell that summer. The knowledge that we could accomplish anything has had an impact on the rest of my life. I believe that the 'summer of 74' got me several job interviews.

After the celebration of completing the journey, life continued as it was before we started the trip. I was a Senior in Wheeling College focusing on my Accounting Degree while working part time at the A&P

(a grocery store) about 20 to 32 hours a week. Jerry, the manager at the A&P was my first mentor. It is amazing how one man could help so many young people grow and accept responsibilities of life. All the while I was still living at home with my mother and my siblings. I was living my life with friends from college, high school and the job, it was a good time for me.

I graduated with a BS in Accounting in May 1975. I started working for Wheeling Machine Products & Co. as a Staff Accountant. This was when I learned the difference between textbook knowledge and how it really worked. It is also when I met my second mentor, John. He taught me how to complete a task to completion with a high degree of perfection.

In the summer of 1975, I met the love of my life. Kim was completing her 'Parks and Recreation' degree from West Virginia University with an internship at Oglebay Park. She lived in a rustic cabin, for the summer, at the park with several other college woman.

Jill was one of her roommates who was KC's fiancée. KC introduced us and that was the beginning of my life. We were married in June 1976 in her hometown of Gary, West Virginia. Once married she continued to work at the park, and we lived in Wheeling West Virginia. I could not have imagined the last 48 years without Kim managing the Gantzer household.

I continued to study accounting with the purpose of passing the CPA Exam, which I passed in May 1978. In July I accepted the position of Staff Accountant at Union Federal Savings and Loan. What a move. I soon found that accounting for banks was different than most corporations. I loved the job and again had a new mentor, Betty. She taught me so much about banking, finance and management that I was so grateful. I was very lucky to have good mentors in my career and to be able to mentor many individuals myself.

Change occurred on March 16, 1982. Kim and I had an 8 lb. 13 oz. baby girl, Lindsay. This was a life changer. We always hear about a child changing a parent, this was the case with us. Lindsay was born with Down Syndrome; the doctors said it was genetic chromosome 21 disorder that would cause developmental and intellectual delays. We were quick to learn that we could adapt many items in her environment to encourage her to grow mentally and physically. It was a success. She graduated from Dublin High School, went to a community college for several years and has held numerous jobs. She is a role model in everything that she has tried to accomplish. She has been accepted as a co-worker and a good friend in all of her endeavors. Now at 42 years old, she is a Personal Trainer for Special Need individuals. As an adult, Lindsay is her mom's and my best friend, we could not be prouder of her lifestyle and accomplishments.

We moved to Dublin, Ohio in 1986 with a Bank transfer and this has been our home since then. This was a great move for all of us, great schools for Lindsay, many challenges and opportunities for Kim and professional development for me. My career continued in the Banking industry the rest of my professional life. I held positions of Controller, CFO, VP Finance and as a member of the Board of Directors at several Community Banks.

I retired in 2014 and have adjusted to a nonstructured life. I also volunteered at the Down Syndrome Association of Central Ohio (DSACO) when we first moved to Ohio. I was the Treasurer when the Association was in its infancy. My contribution was to complete the IRS paperwork to get then qualified as a 501 (c) (3). I also served as the Chairman of Champaign County Lawnview Industries sheltered workshop in Urbana Ohio.

One final comment, this July I was able to celebrate with my nephew, Mike. He and his friend Kurt completed a cross-country bike trip from San Franscisco to Ocean City, Maryland (same start and end points as KC & I did 50 years ago). Mike was 1 year old

when we made our cross-country trip and has always talked about taking the trip. He did it! I was able to relive our trip through their on-line blog and joined them for 32 miles as they traveled through Dublin, Ohio. I could not have been prouder of them.

My congratulations to KC for completing the book. May we both continue to ride our bikes and the experiences of the summer of 1974.

September 1, 2024

ENDNOTES

1. *Hold Me, Thrill Me, Kiss* Me was written by Harry Noble and originally performed by Karen Chandler in 1954. Re-recorded by Mel Carter in 1965 and Gloria Estefan in 1974.

2. Thesiger, Wilfred. Arabian Sands. Penguin Classics, 2008.

3. Meriwether Lewis was in Pittsburgh, PA when he received word that his Virginia next-door neighbor President Thomas Jefferson wanted him to lead an expedition to find a northwest passage to the Pacific Ocean.

4. Water Safety Instructor Certification is a course taught by the American Red Cross that prepares you to teach advanced swimming, water safety, and rescue skills. It is often required to be a lifeguard.

5. *Baywatch* was an NBC television series from 1989 to 2001 about lifeguards dramatically charging into the surf to save people on the beaches of Los Angeles and Hawaii starring David Hasselhoff and Pamela Anderson.

6. *The Long and Winding Road* was written by Paul McCartney and released on the Beatles 1970 Let it Be album in 1970.

7. *Band on the Run* was written by Paul McCartney and released by his new group Wings on their 1973 album titled Band on the Run.

8. *Wild Horses* was written by Mick Jagger and Keith Richards and released on their Rolling Stone's Sticky Fingers album in 1971.

9. Susan Boyles is a Scottish singer with Aspergers syndrome (on the autism spectrum) who became a world-wide sensation when she sang Wild Horses on the Britain's Got Talent variety television show in 2009.

10. Muir, John, "The Grand Cañon Of The Colorado." (1902). John Muir: A Reading Bibliography by Kimes (Muir articles 1866-1986). 278. https://scholarlycommons.pacific.edu/jmb/278

11. California Crimes and Accidents Associated with Hitchhiking. California Highway Patrol Operational Analysis Section. 1974.

12. Max Quotes. Max Neumegen. 21 April 2020. www.maxneumegentraveller.org

13. Myalgia is the medical term for muscle pain from the Greek 'myos'(muscle) and 'algos'(pain)

14. Watergate was a botched attempt by 5 burglars to rob the Democratic National Committee offices in the Watergate Office Building. The robbery was funded by the Nixon (Republican) re-election campaign, with Nixon's knowledge.

15. *You Can Always Come Home* was written by Alan Jackson and inspired by his daughter going off to college. It was released in 2015 on his album Angels and Alcohol.

PHOTO CREDITS

Unless listed below, all photos were taken by either KC or Bob in 1974.

Front Pages

The Route Sketch of our route was created and photographed by KC 2024.

Photo of "Reader's Rock" taken by KC, 2024.

1974

KC and Bob on Bicycles. Photo from Wheeling Intelligencer newspaper August 1974, by Andy Leheny.

Ocean Park Motel Post Card. Photo by Mike Roberts, Berkeley, California. Circa1974.

Ode to Thomas Stevens

Thomas Stevens photo. Unknown author - Image from Around the world on a bicycle (London: Sampson Low, Marston, Searle and Rivington, 1887) by Thomas Stevens: https://archive.org/details/cu31924023253093.

Thomas Stevens's Bicycle Journey Around the World by Dravot Benutzer based on Image:BlankMap-World-1872.png by Astrokey44, https://commons.wikimedia.org/wiki/Commons:GNU_Free_Documentation_License,_version_1.2

Beatles to Beetles and Ghost Towns

Mountain Pine Beetle. Image is a work of the Forest Service of the United States Department of Agriculture. As a work of the U.S. federal government, the image is in the public domain.

Dam Luck and a Crash in Santa Claus

Naegleria fowleri Life Cycle This image is a work of the ***Centers for Disease Control and Prevention****, part of the* ***United States Department of Health and Human Services****, taken or made as part of an employee's official duties. As a work of the U.S. federal government, the image is in the* ***public domain****. From* File:Naegleria fowleri lifecycle stages.JPG - Wikimedia Commons

Almost Alamosa

Sketch of clincher and sew-up tire cross-sections created and photographed by KC, 2024.

A Madonna Encounter and a Melanoplus Attack

Madonna of the Trail, Council Grove, Kansas. Image listed on the National Register of Historic Places in the United States of America. Reference number 100002245. Photo by Joe Carmel 26 May 2006.

Melanoplus spretus. By Julius Bien - Annual report of the Agricultural Experiment Station of the University of Minnesota. (11th July 1902-June 1903) (secondary source, Biodiversity Heritage Library: plate, caption), Public Domain, https://commons.wikimedia.org/w/index.php?curid=20371856

Brotherhood and Pedaling Home Without Dick

Photo of journal page with front page headline from unknown newspaper in Columbus, Ohio, August 9, 1974.

You Can Always Go Home

Mingo Indian atop Wheeling Hill. Photo circa 1930's Courtesy the Ohio County Public Library Archives, Wheeling, WV.

Photo of Circa 1954 Lou W Nau photo, photographer unknown, courtesy of Jeffrey L Nau.

Photo of Circa 2024 Lou W Nau Inc. From The Intelligencer November 21, 2017, by Jessica Broverman.

Nearing the Finish. Photo from Wheeling Intelligencer newspaper August 1974, by Andy Leheny.

Appalachians and Appaloosas

A boat on the C&O Canal, circa 1900-1924. E.B. Thompson, photographer - National Park Service Historic Photograph Collection; E.B. Thompson Collection. Catalog No. HPC-000060.

Harpers Ferry photo from Maryland Heights. Public domain downloaded from https://wvtourism.com Harpers Ferry-rs-8068-edited-2048x1277.jpg (2048×1277)

Deviantly Crossing the Finish Line

Chesapeake Bay Bridge photo by Brycia James, September 19, 2017.

Greetings from Ocean City Post Card. Photo by F.W. Brueckmann. Circa 1974.

REFERENCES and FURTHER READING RESOURCES

Chapter 1: 1974

Reid, Carlton. Bike Boom: The Unexpected Resurgence of Cycling. Washington DC, Island Press., 2017.

Cuthbertson, Tom. Anybody's Bike Book. Ten Speed Press, 1985.

Ballantine, Richard. Richards Bicycle Book. Pan Books, 1983.

Coyle, Daniel. Lance Armstrong: Tour de Force. Harpersport. 2006.

De Vise, Daniel. The Comeback: Greg LeMond the True King of American Cycling. Atlantic Monthly Press, 5 June 2018.

Selective Service System. The Vietnam Lotteries. History and Records. https://www.sss.gov/history-and-records/vietnam-lotteries/. Accessed 7 July 2024.

Chapter 2: Ode to Thomas Stevens

Stevens, Thomas. Around the World on a Bicycle. Macha Press, 6 September 2016.

Strasser, Christopher. Strasser's Road. Octane Press, 2019.
Stutzman, Paul. Biking Across America. Revell, 2013.

Chapter 3: Lost and Bonking Already?

Kephart, Horace. Camping and Woodcraft (Legacy Edition). Doublebit Press, 2019.

Chapter 4: General Delivery

Lonard, Devin. Neither Snow nor Rain: History of the US Postal Service. Grove Press, 2021.

Goldner, Kathryn and Carole Vogel. Humphrey, the Wrong Way Whale. Dillon Press, 1987.

Chapter 5: You Go That Way-I'll Go This Way

DeVoto, Bernard, editor. The Journals of Lewis and Clark. Houghton Mifflin Co., 1953.

Sullivan, Kevin. The Bundy Murders: A Comprehensive History. McFarland, 2020.

Davis, Don. The Jeffrey Dahmer Story- An American Nightmare. St Martin Press, 1995.

Gisela, K. John Wayne Gacy: The Killer Clown. Grizzly Books, 2021.

Chapter 6: Beatles to Beetles and Ghost Towns

Barkley, Yvonne. "Everything you have always wanted to know about bark beetles but were afraid to ask." University of Idaho Extension Forestry Information Series II. Insects and Diseases, no. 26 (1996).

USDA Forest Service Rocky Mountain Region and Rocky Mountain Research Station. Review of the Forest Service Response: The Bark Beetle Outbreak in Northern Colorado and Southern Wyoming. September 2011. https://www.fs.usda.gov/Internet/FSE_DOCUMENTS/stelprdb5340736.pdf Accessed 7 July 2024.

Muir, John. The Yosemite. Binker North. 1912.

Womack, Kenneth. Long and Winding Roads: Evolving Artistry of the Beatles. Bloomsbury Academic, 2023.

Chapter 7: Trapped in Tonopah

Hill, Shawn. A Guide to Ghost Towns and Mining Camps of Nye County, NV. Dodd Mead & Co,1981.

Peter Merlin. Tonopah Test Range. Arcadia Publishing, 2021.

Chapter 8: Nye...It was a Stampede!

American Wild Horse Conservation. A compendium of papers and publications describing the governmental mishandling of wild horses. www.americanwildhorse.org Accessed 4 July 2024.

Philipps, David. Wild Horse Country: The History, Myth, and Future of the Mustang. WW Norton & Co., 2017.

Chapter 9: Dam Luck and a Crash in Santa Claus

Center for Disease Control. Naeglaria fowleri infection. contains up to date information for the public and professionals on this infective organism. https://cdc.gov/naegleria Accessed 3 August 2024.

Hiltzik, Michael. Colossus: The Turbulent, Thrilling Saga of the Building of Hoover Dam. Free Press, 2011.

McBride, Pete. The Colorado River: Chasing Water. Rizzoli, 2024.

Chapter 10: More Water Rights and Wrongs and a Desert Warning

Powell, James. Dead Pool: Lake Powell, Global warming, and the Future of Water in the West. University of California Press, 2009.

Skinner, Anna. "Could Lake Mead Be Saved by Sacrificing Lake Powell?" Newsweek, 8 February 2023.

Chapter 11: Trust and Risk

Chesters, Graeme and David Smith. "The Neglected Art of Hitch- hiking: Risk, Trust and Sustainability". Sociological Research Online, vol. 6, no. 3, 2001. http://www.socresonline.org.uk/6/3/chesters.html

Chapter 12: Navajo Regrets and a Colorado Catastrophe

Tony Hillerman wrote a series of 18 detective mystery books from 1970-2006 published by Harper. They feature Navajo police characters Leaphorn, Chee and Manuelito (adapted as TV series Dark Winds in 2022). His writings immerse the reader in Navajo Nation landscape and culture and have won multiple awards.

Blackhawk, Ned. The Rediscovery of America: Native Peoples and the Unmaking of US History. Yale University Press, 2023.

Coates, Ta-Nehisi. Between the World and Me. One World. 2015.

Diangelo, Robin. White Fragility: Why it's so hard for white people to talk about racism. Beacon Press, 2018.

Locke, Raymond. The Book of the Navajo. Mankind Publ. Co., 5th edition, 1992.

Chapter 13: Almost Alamosa

Gonzales, Laurence. Deep Survival: Who Lives, Who Dies, and Why. WH Norton & Co. Inc., 2003.

Brandt, Jobst. The Bicycle Wheel. Avocet Press, 1988. More than you would ever want to know about the theory and mechanics of building a bicycle wheel.

Chapter 14: Mascots and Sunsets

McMillin, Sue. "Lamar High School drops "Savage" from its mascot name as 10 new schools are found in violation of state law". The Colorado Sun. 20 May 2022. https://coloradosun.com Accessed 21 June 2024.

Rosso, Mike. "The Fryingpan-Arkansas River Project at 50". Colorado Central Magazine. 1 June 2012. https://www.coloradocentral-magazine.com Accessed 14 August 2024.

John E. Thorson et al., Dividing Western Waters: A Century of Adjudicating Rivers and Streams, 8 University of Denver Water Law Review. 355 (2005).

Chapter 15: A Madonna Encounter and a Melanoplus Attack

Davis, Linda. August Leimbach (1882-1965)- Find a Grave Memorial. https://www.findagrave.com/memorial/208896315/august_leimbach Accessed 22 May 2024.

Shapiro, Mary. "Madona of the Trail: Norman Karl of Webster Groves is proud to tout the life & art of his famous grandfather, sculptor & teacher August Leimbach". Webster-Kirkwood Times. 9 September 2016.

Lockwood, J . Locust: The Devastating Rise and Mysterious Disappearance of the Insect that Shaped the American Frontier. Basic Books, 2004.

Chapter 16: Garbage, silos, and Seeking Salvation in Sedalia

Fransen, Steve. "Silos". https://forages.oregonstste.edu/oregon/topics/storage/silos# Accessed 12 September 2024.

Sedalia-Missouri Cowtown. Legends of America. https://www.ledgendsofamerica.com/sedalia-missouri Accessed 20 August 2024.

Chapter 17: Goose Liver, Cemetery Dreams and Big Dreams

Eggener, Keith. Cemeteries. WW Norton & Co., 2010.

Vespa, Maggie. "Sleeping by the Dead: The battle over homeless camps near a cemetery in Lents". KGW8. August

10, 2018. https://www.kgw.com/article/sleeping-by-the-dead-one-neighborhoods-battle-over-homeless-camps-and-a-cemetery/283-582495875 Accessed 12 August 2014.

Lisa Bortolotti, editor. Delusions in Context. Palgrave Macmillan, 2018.

Chapter 18: Brotherhood and Pedaling Home Without Dick

Kingkade, Tyler. "Sigma Alpha Epsilon Bans Pledging Nationwide in Effort to Stop Hazing". HuffPost, March 11, 2014. https://www.huffpost.com/entry/sigma-alpha-epsilon-pledging-hazing_n_4938425/amp . Accessed 10 August 2024.

Marshall, Max. Among the Bros: A Fraternity Crime Story. Harper, 2023. Book about the dark side of Kappa Alpha fraternity and fraternity ethos gone wrong.

Stone, Roger and Mike Colapietro. Tricky Dick: The Rise and Fall and Rise of Richard M. Nixon. Skyhorse, 2017.

Chapter 19: You Can Always Go Home

Heat-Moon, William. River-Horse: Logbook of a Boat Across America. Penguin Books, 1999.

Appleman, Roy. Lewis and Clark's Transcontinental Exploration 1804-1806. Jefferson National Parks Association, 3rd edition, 2000.

Hartman, Marcia. "McColloch's Leap and Other Wheeling Wayside Adventures". The Crossroads, vol 6 Issue 6, 2021. https://www.archivingwheeling.org/blog/mccollochs-leap-and-other-wheeling-wayside-adventures Accessed 12 June 2024.

Chapter 20: Appalachians and Appaloosas

Hendricks, Mark. The Central Appalachians: Mountains of the Chesapeake. Schiffer, 2024. A collection of essays and photographs about biodiversity, adventure and ecology in the mountains of West Virginia, Virginia, Maryland and Pennsylvania.

High, Mike. The C&O Canal Companion: A Journey through Potomac History. Johns Hopkins University Press, 2015.

C&O Canal Trust. Nonprofit partner with the National Park Service. Manages canal quarter rentals, volunteer programs, and canal town partnerships. www.canaltrust.org

Chapter 21: Deviantly Crossing the Finish Line

Sedlar, Nedjc, Amy Irwin, Douglas Martin, Ruby Roberts. A qualitative systematic review on the application of the normalization of deviance phenomenon within high-risk industries. Journal of Safety Research 84 (2023) 290-305.

Paulson, John and Erin Paulson. The Chesapeake Bay Bridge. Arcadia Publishing, 2019.

Great Chesapeake Bay Swim. Bay Swim Archives Online. Bay swim results by years. https://bayswim.awardspace.info/past_finishers.html

ACKNOWLEDGEMENTS

My sincere thanks to my parents Richard Louis Nau and Sarah Jane Nau who provided me life's compass and a quest for knowledge. Their trust and the freedom to explore and take risks was a gift far greater than they ever knew.

To the people I encountered on this journey - you taught me lessons that endured for fifty years.

To my writer heroes Alison Wearing of Memoir Writers Ink and the inspiring folks in the Portland Writer's Workshop who shared the tools of their trade, especially Dan Siger, Kristy Schnabel, and Chris Sullivan.

To my Oregon neighbor and copy editor Nancy - who tells it like it is.

To my children Ryan, Mike, and Kristen for your subtle encouragement as I wrote this book, and for making homes where your parents and your children can warmly return.

To my wife Peggy, who gives me the space to write, the feedback that I need, and the love that launches me. Words cannot express what you mean to me.

And finally, to Bob Gantzer. It has been my privilege to relive and reflect on our summer of 1974. As I wrote in my journal so long ago, "To travel alone, we'd never make it. To travel with Bob - who couldn't.

About The Author

Konrad C. Nau

Konrad (KC) Nau is the son of a plumber and was raised along with his six siblings in Wheeling, West Virginia. He graduated from Bethany College, West Virginia in 1975 with a degree in biology. He attended medical school at the West Virginia University School of Medicine from 1975-1979 and completed his residency in Family Medicine at WVU Hospital in Morgantown, West Virginia in 1982. He then started a small family practice clinic in doctorless Harpers Ferry, West Virginia along with classmate Rosemarie Cannarella, MD. After twelve years of private practice including clinic, hospital, and obstetrical care they joined the faculty of the WVU Department of Family Medicine and established the WVU Rural Family Medicine Residency Program in Harpers Ferry, West Virginia. This educational enterprise grew into what is now the Eastern Division of the West Virginia University School of Medicine. Nau served various roles including Department Chair, Vice-President for Medical Affairs, and CEO of University Healthcare Physicians. His final five years were as Regional Campus Dean. In 2017 he retired from WVU and returned to the private practice of family medicine with Glenwood Medical Associates in

Glenwood Springs, Colorado.

The cross-country bicycle journey spurred him on to many more endurance-type pursuits including the Boston Marathon, the Great Chesapeake Bay Swim, and the Hawaiian Ironman, but none were more memorable than the summer of 1974. He is the father of two sons by his first marriage, and one stepdaughter by his current marriage. He retired from medicine in 2024 and lives part-time in Glenwood Springs, Colorado and part-time in Cannon Beach, Oregon, with his wife Peggy. Together they cherish their two dogs, Bella and Mia, and their ten grandchildren.

Dr. Nau has authored several medical journal articles and monographs. "I Rode a Bike for 50 Years" is his first novel. He still rides a bike.

www.ingramcontent.com/pod-product-compliance
Lightning Source LLC
Chambersburg PA
CBHW070023100426
42740CB00013B/2581
* 9 7 9 8 9 9 1 7 7 9 5 0 0 *